The Vatersay Raiders

The Vatersay Raiders

Ben Buxton

BIRLINN

*To the memory of John MacInnes (1946—2003) of Edinburgh,
whose painstaking research into his ancestors in Berneray and Barra
revealed much new information on the Barra Isles, which, it is
hoped, will one day be published*

First published in 2008 by
Birlinn Limited
West Newington House
10 Newington Road
Edinburgh
EH9 1QS

www.birlinn.co.uk

Copyright © Ben Buxton 2008
Reprinted 2011

The moral right of Ben Buxton to be identified
as the author of this work has been asserted by him in
accordance with the Copyright, Designs and Patents Act 1988

All rights reserved. No part of this publication may be
reproduced, stored or transmitted in any form without
the express written permission of the publisher.

ISBN 978 1 84158 553 6

British Library Cataloguing-in-Publication Data
A catalogue record for this book is available from the British Library

Typeset by Hewer Text UK Ltd, Edinburgh
Printed and bound in the UK by CPI

Contents

Appendices:

List of Illustrations and Maps

Illustrations

1. View of Castle Bay, Barra, and the islands to the south.
2. Lady Gordon Cathcart.
3. The herring curing station on Bàgh Bhatarsaigh in the 1870s.
4. The eastern end of the herring station.
5. The raiders' huts on the site of the present township of Vatersay, in September 1908.
6. As above, looking towards Barra.
7. The ten Vatersay raiders, with their two legal advisers.
8. Vatersay Township in 1927.
9. Vatersay House and Township in 1948.
10. The eastern part of Vatersay Township in 1949.
11. Vatersay Township in 2006.
12. The ruins of Vatersay House, 2006.
13. Bringing home the hay across the machair in 1948.

Maps

Foreword and acknowledgements

'Vatersay may yet become a place famous in history,' claimed a newspaper writer in February 1906. This prediction turned out to be prophetic: Vatersay did become famous, more so than other cases of land being raided by land-hungry cottars. One hundred years on, the raiders remain famous in Vatersay and Barra, but other raiders of farms in Barra have long been forgotten. The Vatersay raiders are regarded as heroes in their own island, having fought for and won the land still occupied by their descendants.

It is something of a paradox that, having been so well known at the time, the remarkable story of the raiders has never been told in any detail in print. Various authors have included the raiding of Vatersay in accounts of the Barra Isles or in wider studies of land raiding and crofting. These authors have had access to the voluminous records of the Congested Districts Board and the Scottish Office, but because of the vast amount of documentation, they have seen only some of them. While researching among them for this book, I became aware of deficiencies in my own account in *Mingulay, an island and its people* (Birlinn, 1995). Even now, I cannot claim to have seen all the records, but, using other sources such as newspaper articles, oral history, and the work of authors who have had access to other archives, I am hopeful that my account is accurate. I have had to be selective in what I have used in the chapters on the raiding and settlement, also in the brief account of the subsequent history.

Being non-resident I have not been able to make full use of the vast amount of knowledge among the present people of Vatersay and Barra, and being a non-Gaelic speaker, I have not been able to make full use of the tape recordings of past inhabitants made by the School of Scottish Studies in Edinburgh. I hope that, some day, somebody may make more use of these than I have.

I was inspired to write this book because I felt it was important to document the story of the raiders, particularly because of the approaching centenary of the raiding and settlement. I also felt that the book should include the earlier history of the island, about which very little has been written (apart from the pre-history, which has been investigated, and I have therefore not covered it in detail), and I have outlined developments since the community was established.

Once again I must record my thanks to the people of Vatersay and Barra for their help and support. I am particularly indebted to Mary Kate MacKinnon, and I am also grateful to the following: Donald Duncan and Peggy Ann Campbell; Rhoda Campbell, Morag MacDougall, Michael MacKinnon; Hector MacLeod; Neil MacDonald; Calum MacNeil; Teresa MacNeil; Margaret Nixon.

I am also very grateful to the following for assistance in various ways: Dr Colleen Batey, University of Glasgow; Professor Keith Branigan, University of Sheffield; Edwina Burridge, Inverness Library; Dr Ewen Cameron, University of Edinburgh; Michael Clark; Professor David Gilbertson; Paul Harding; Andrew Kerr; Bill Lawson; Dr Cathlin Macaulay, School of Scottish Studies Archives; Alastair MacEachan; Paul McGuire; Linda MacKinnon, Castlebay Library; Fiona MacLeod, Highland Archives; Dr Nicola Mills; Andrew Nicoll, Scottish Catholic Archives; Dr Richard Pankhurst, Botanic Garden, Edinburgh; Magdalena Sagarzazu, Canna Archives; Dr Anke-Beate Stahl; Brian Wilson; Maggie Wilson, National Museums of Scotland Enterprises.

The following kindly read drafts of the book and I am most grateful to them for their invaluable comments and suggestions: Caroline Buxton, Dr Ewen Cameron, Mary Kate MacKinnon, Flora MacLeod, Eve Sheldon, Patrick Tolfree. I am of course responsible for any errors.

For permission to reproduce material I am grateful to the following: Canna Archives, National Trust for Scotland, plate 10; Comunn Eachdraidh Bharraigh agus Bhatarsaigh, front cover (by RMR Milne) and plates 4, 7, 14; Donald Duncan and Peggy Ann Campbell, plate 20; Robin Linzee Gordon, plate 2; Mary Ann MacDougall, plate 18; Morag MacDougall, John MacDougall's account; Neil MacDonald, plates 24, 25; Peggy MacNeil, plate 16; Teresa MacNeil, letters of Neil MacPhee; National Archives of Scotland, plates 5, 6, AF42/5318; The Trustees of the National Museums of Scotland, plates 9, 13, 22, 23, 27; National Trust for Scotland, plates 29, 30, 31 (RMR Milne Album); School of Scottish Studies, plate 15, and extracts from recordings of Nan MacKinnon published in *Tocher*; Scottish Catholic Archives, plate 3; Lisa Storey, translation of John MacDougall's account. Plates 33 and 34 are by Dom Odo Blundell. Plates 1, 11, 12, 17, 19, 21, 26, 28, 32 are by Ben Buxton.

Notes to readers:

In Vatersay and Barra the term 'the raiders' is used to refer to all those who settled on Vatersay illegally between 1906 and 1908. In this book I use the term for those pioneers who raided in the first year or so, of whom ten were imprisoned. I also use the term for those who raided Vatersay in the years before 1906.

Place-names: for Vatersay and Sandray names which are on the 2003 edition of the Ordnance Survey Explorer map 452, I have used the forms given on that map. Many Vatersay place-names are not on the map, and some of those which are, are inaccurately located. For names in Barra and elsewhere I have used the Anglicised forms in common usage in print, and given Gaelic versions in Appendix 7.

References: to keep reference numbers to a minimum, numbers at the end of paragraphs give references for that paragraph, and in some cases, previous paragraphs. References are not given where the source is quoted in the text.

Prologue: 'An extraordinary proceeding'

It is 2 June 1908. Ten fishermen from the small island of Vatersay in the Outer Hebrides present themselves before the Court of Session in Edinburgh charged with breach of interdict (injunction) and contempt of court. Their alleged crime: they had refused to leave the island which they had raided – in other words invaded – and on which they had built huts and planted potatoes without the permission of the landowner.

The raiders were from the nearby islands of Barra and Mingulay where they had lived in primitive and overcrowded conditions. They were cottars, that is, people with no crofts (smallholdings) for growing food or grazing their cattle, and some had only makeshift houses. For years the raiders from Barra had appealed to the landowner, Lady Cathcart, for crofts on Vatersay. At the time, the island was run as a single farm, inhabited only by the farmer and his workers. Her Ladyship, who lived in Cluny Castle in Aberdeenshire, and had not visited her island dominions since 1878, had consistently refused requests for crofts on Vatersay, so, in desperation, the raiders had taken the law into their own hands. There had been no violence at any time – although the raiders had acted in a threatening way towards the farmer – nor had there been any police or government action to remove them.

The men had invaded Vatersay in July 1906, and over the following months took up residence. Lady Cathcart had served interdicts on the men, requiring them to leave the island, in April 1907. However, she had delayed further action in order to give them time to leave, and she was in negotiation with the Scottish Office about creating a crofting settlement on the island. She was also in dispute with the Scottish Office because it had refused to take action to remove the raiders. The raiders had defied the interdicts and settlers continued to arrive, undeterred by the threat of legal action. In January 1908, Lady Cathcart served a complaint for breach of interdict and contempt of court on the men.

The trial was to have been on 19 May, but the raiders had written to the court beforehand saying that they did not have the money for their fares, so the case was postponed until 2 June. They added in the letter, 'we did not wish to defy the court . . . we have every respect for the court but not for our landlord or her advisors . . . she is not to blame so much as they are for she has not been here for 30 years and does not know our real condition.'

There were elements of farce to the raiders' journey to Edinburgh by steamer and train. To begin with, their fares were paid by their adversary, Lady Cathcart. It is unlikely that any of them had been to the capital before, although they would have been to fishing ports on the east coasts of Scotland and England; unlikely, too, that any of them had been on a train before. They arrived in Edinburgh the evening before their court appearance, but missed the reception party awaiting them. *The Edinburgh Evening News* of 2 June reported:

Owing to some miscarriage in the arrangements their arrival was quieter than otherwise it might have been. The party of ten was due to reach Princes Street Station at 9.27 pm. When the train came in, the 300 or so persons on the platform were disappointed to find that no Barra men were on the train . . . the men had got into the wrong portion of the train at Larbert and had been carried to the Waverley Station. Mr Donald Shaw, their law agent, and several members of the committee formed to look after the interests of the Barra men immediately repaired to the Waverley Station to welcome the squatters. Few persons were in the station, but a cheer was raised as the blueclad fishermen made for their quarters in High Street.

It is remarkable that the sight of ten fishermen in the station was so unusual that ordinary members of the public realised who they were, and it shows that there was a lot of press coverage in advance of the trial.

At the trial the next day,

the proceedings excited a considerable amount of public interest. The courtroom was packed to overflowing, while a large number of spectators overlooked the scene from the galleries above. The squatters were accommodated in a seat immediately behind the reporting bench. A bronzed and hardy lot they looked in their seafaring garb, the respectability of which certainly did not suggest dire poverty.

Counsel for Lady Cathcart put the case for the complainer. He stated that the men had breached the interdict served on them by the court, had continued to occupy the land, and intended to continue to do so. The only previous case where a respondent for breach of interdict had taken up that position was in 1887, and this led to his imprisonment.

Counsel for the men, Arthur Dewar, stated that 'they admitted that they had gone to Vatersay without the authority of the complainer, and that they had failed to obey the order of the court.' He wished to dispel the impression given in some quarters and in the press, that 'the respondents were reckless and unprincipled men who had wantonly seized the property of a benevolent landlord, notwithstanding all the benefits they had received throughout their lives.' As evidence of the true situation he quoted from the report by Sheriff Wilson, who had failed in an attempt to persuade the raiders to leave Vatersay the previous year. In conclusion, he said,

> They had been driven by the system and circumstances they were powerless to control into disobedience. The disobedience was not due to disrespect, but entirely to their environment. The respondents had asked him to express the hope that those who

could reform the law should take note of what they
had had to suffer, and so alter the law that they might
have the opportunity of becoming once more law-
abiding citizens. There was an outburst of applause at
the conclusion of the speech. The ushers immediately
called for silence, and the Lord Justice Clerk char-
acterised the applause as 'most unseemly.'

The Lord Justice Clerk, having established from Mr Dewar that
the men intended to continue to defy the court by remaining in
Vatersay, delivered judgement. He said that the background to
the case was

not material for the court at all . . . In view of all that had
been said about not dealing harshly with such ignorant
men, the sentence to be pronounced on them would be a
limited one. It was right to give warning that if the breach
was continued after the expiry of the sentence the case
could not be dealt with as it was being dealt with now. The
sentence pronounced was two months imprisonment upon
each of the respondents. The crofters, who had the terms of
the sentence interpreted to them in Gaelic by their solicitor, accepted the situation stolidly. After the sentence was
pronounced they retired to one of the side rooms in
Parliament House and partook of refreshments. The intention was to have them removed to the Calton Prison in
the ordinary prison van, but Mr Donald Shaw, their agent,
objected, and offered to provide another conveyance.
Shortly after three o'clock they were removed in cabs.

Three prisoners and a policeman were in each cab. As each batch emerged into the square a cheer was raised, and they were exhorted to keep up their courage by persons in the crowd. They all appeared to be in good spirits, and smilingly acknowledged the greetings of the crowd.

How did this 'extraordinary proceeding', as a newspaper writer put it, come about? This book sets out to tell the story of the background to these events, starting with the earliest human occupation of Vatersay, and bringing the account up to date with the more recent history.

1. Early times

Vatersay, 'Bhatarsaigh' in Gaelic, lies at the southern end of the Outer Hebrides or Western Isles. It is the first, and the largest, of a chain of five small islands to the south of Barra. It is only 200 metres from Barra at the narrowest point of the Sound of Vatersay, and Sandray, Pabbay, Mingulay and Berneray are strung out to the south-west. These islands, together with Barra and some islands off its north-east coast, are known as the Barra Isles. They make up the parish of Barra, which was described in 1847 as 'composed of a cluster of islands surrounded by a boisterous sea, making the passage from one island to another a matter of very considerable hazard.' Since 1912 Vatersay has been the most southerly inhabited island in the Outer Hebrides, for people from the islands to the south raided and settled there between 1907 and 1912, leaving their more distant islands deserted.

Vatersay measures about five kilometres (three miles) east–west by a slightly shorter distance north–south. It is highly irregular in shape, consisting of northern and southern hilly parts, joined by a low sandy isthmus only about 400 metres wide at its narrowest point, flanked on either side by magnificent beaches of white shell sand. These beaches are the most notable physical feature of the island according to today's tastes, but in the past the eastern bay, Bàgh Bhatarsaigh, is the feature most often mentioned by early writers, being one of the best natural harbours in the Outer Hebrides. From the sea, Vatersay looks like two islands, which, some thousands of years ago, it was.

The geologist John MacCulloch described Vatersay in 1816 thus: 'This island consists of two green hills, united by a low sandy bar where the opposite seas nearly meet. Indeed if the sea did not perpetually supply fresh sand to replace what the wind carries off, it would very soon form two islands; nor would the tenant have much cause for surprise if, on getting up some morning, he required a boat to milk his cows. The whole island is in a state of perpetual revolution, from the alternate accumulation and dispersion of sand-hills; which at least affords the pleasure of variety.'

The isthmus, Meallaich in Gaelic, is technically a tombolo, or sand bar joining two islands. In MacCulloch's day it seems to have been bare sand, but in time vegetation began to colonise it and it became machair, the rich grassland of the west coasts (mainly) of the Outer Hebrides, which supports a profusion of wild flowers in summer. The machair extends south to the southern beach, Bàgh a' Deas, and eighteenth-century maps show that this area was also sandy at that time. From 1850 it was the arable land of Vatersay Farm, and since 1909 it has been the croft lands of Vatersay Township. There are two other areas of machair: east of Caraigrigh on the Uidh peninsula, and at Caolas, between Traigh Bhàrlais and Port a' Bhàta. Many of the early accounts of Vatersay mention its fertility.

Recent research has shown that the tombolo began to develop about 7,000 years ago, when sea level was several metres lower, and it may not have become a permanent fixture, above high-tide level, for some time. During its history there have been periods of growth, stability and erosion. In its present form, therefore, Vatersay is a very young island. In contrast to the isthmus, the rest of the island is composed of rounded hills of Lewisian Gneiss, the rock of all the Outer Hebrides, which at nearly three thousand million years old is amongst the oldest rock on earth. The hills, rising to 190 metres (625 feet) are partly covered with rough grassland and heath, some of it peaty, but there is a good deal of bare rock. In places there is glacial till, a legacy of the ice sheet which covered the islands during the last ice age. There are no trees, and no large streams. There are a few very tiny lochs, so small that they hardly merit the term. A writer in 1845 described sea-caves on the west side of the island which had been used for storing smuggled goods.[1]

Topographically, Vatersay has more in common with Sandray than with the three other islands to the south. Unlike these three, they have no sea cliffs of any height. Many areas of the coastline are low-lying and were settled, in contrast to the others where settlement sites were more limited. Sandray is under a kilometre (half a mile) south of Vatersay. It is roughly circular, and up to about three kilometres (two miles) across. The interior rises to two peaks, the highest being Càrn Ghaltair, 207 metres (678 feet) high. In historical terms, too, Vatersay and Sandray were closely linked. After Sandray's crofting population was evicted in 1835 it was used as grazing by Vatersay Farm, and since 1909, when both islands were bought by the state, it has continued to serve that function for the crofters of the southern townships of Vatersay. Vatersay and Sandray were more closely connected culturally, as well as physically, to Barra.

The claim made in 1906 that 'Vatersay may yet become a place famous in history' turned out to be prophetic: it gained national attention over the raiding and settlement by people from neighbouring islands later in 1906 and the following years. It became, in another writer's words, 'the theatre upon which was fought one of the keenest conflicts in the struggle for land reform in the Hebrides.' This period is documented in detail in the form of records and newspaper reports. Vatersay had previously been in the news in 1853, when the *Annie Jane* was wrecked and about 400 emigrants were drowned. Otherwise, before the twentieth century, the outside world took little interest in the island and its history is not well documented. There are very few visitors' accounts; it did not have the spectacular cliff scenery and birdlife or the remoteness of Mingulay, for instance. While it is mentioned in many books and articles, there are very few articles devoted to the island. From the scanty evidence, we can piece together something of Vatersay's history from 1549, when it is first mentioned, until the raids began in 1900, and then the story of the raiders can be told in much more detail. For the earlier history and prehistory we rely on archaeology and on what is known about the Barra Isles as a whole.

The Barra Isles, and the Outer Hebrides generally, may have been first colonised by small groups of hunter gatherers about

6000 BC, but the earliest definite evidence of occupation in Barra dates to about 3600 BC. This is the site of a Neolithic dwelling, whose inhabitants practised agriculture, at Allt Easdal on the south coast opposite Vatersay. The islands were rather different at that time: sea levels were several metres lower so there was a greater land area, and, in contrast to today's bleak and treeless landscape, they were wooded. Vatersay would have been inhabited then, too; the sound separating it from Barra would have been narrower, and in any case the sea was a highway rather than the barrier it became in more recent times. Vatersay was probably still two islands at that time, as the isthmus may not have become a permanent feature.

Finding evidence of the early settlers is difficult: rising sea levels since the end of the last ice age about 10,000 years ago (which separated Vatersay from Barra by the flooding of what became the Sound of Vatersay) have drowned the coastlines where people are likely to have been living. In some places inland sites and landscapes have been buried under peat or wind-blown sand. The archaeology of the Barra Isles was investigated systematically for the first time during the 1990s by archaeologists from Sheffield University. They found a large number of buildings, monuments and other structures of all periods and of many periods, in other words, sites where building stones have been reused over time. Certain types of prehistoric monuments are found only in the Barra Isles, and in some cases only on some of the islands. It is often difficult to identify what appear to be grass-covered piles or settings of stones with certainty, since such sites could be anything from 5,500 to 100 years old.

Several sites on Vatersay date to the later Neolithic period, between about 3000 and 2000 BC. One is a passage grave, a variety of chambered tomb, on the eastern slopes of Beinn Orosaigh, Caolas. Only the stones of the passage and burial chamber remain, the cairn which once covered it having been removed. Neolithic pottery was found eroding out of a midden (or rubbish dump) on the eastern side of the islet of Bioruaslum, off the west coast of Vatersay, a site presumably occupied for its defensive nature. Also on the islet is a stone-built structure resembling a chambered tomb. Pottery, possibly of Neolithic date, was found in a midden on the south side of Traigh Bhàrlais, Caolas.

There are various 'ritual' or funerary monuments of the late Neolithic and Bronze Age periods, roughly 3000–1500 BC. An arc of stones may be part of a possible stone circle on the western slopes of Am Meall overlooking Eorasdail. There are three possible standing stones, only one of which is still standing: this is a 1.8-metre high stone, forming one side of the entrance of a more recent enclosure on the eastern slopes of Beinn Ruilibreac, so it is possible that it is not of great antiquity. An apparently fallen stone lies in a gap between sections of a massive earth bank, of unknown date, which runs north–south across South Vatersay east of the summit of Beinn Cuidhir. The third possible fallen standing stone is fifteen metres from the shore at Beannachan.

During the period 2000–1000 BC, in the Bronze Age, each island appears to have had variations of types of burial cairns. Vatersay has by far the largest number – twenty nine – of 'kerbed cairns' in the Barra Isles. These cairns are mounds of stones enclosed by a ring of large stones lying horizontally, forming a kerb to the cairn. They are found in groups or cemeteries, one particularly striking group of nine being located in the formerly cultivated area on the north side of Bàgh Siar, west of Treasabhaig. These cairns, with some others nearby, are the only such cairns in North Vatersay. Two cairns in South Vatersay were excavated by Sheffied University archaeologists, one on the west side of the hill crowned by Dun Bhatarsaigh, and one further west. The cairns had been built in a complex way, and contained cremated human bone and peat ash, brought from cremation pyres somewhere else. In one, the eastern cairn, an unfinished stone ard (plough), an unfinished stone axe head, a stone rubber for grinding grain on a quern, and half a bronze cloak fastener were found. It also contained a long stone slab which may previously have been a standing stone, and this has been erected in the middle of the restored cairn.

Only a few sites of dwelling houses of the Bronze Age population have been identified, but several habitation sites dating to the Iron Age, roughly 500 BC to AD 500, are known. Round houses and wheelhouses were the dwellings of the majority of the population. They had low walls of stone, with, presumably, thatched conical roofs. About twenty have been identified, all but two on North Vatersay. Wheelhouses have lengths of walling radiating out from the hearth in the open area at the centre, like the spokes of a wheel. Four, all on North Vatersay, have been identified. The chapel of Cille Bhrianain on Uinessan may have been built on the site of an Iron Age house, as pottery of that period has been found on the mound on which it is built. Although it is impossible to know how many of these houses were inhabited at any one time, Vatersay seems to have been well-populated during this period.

There are two brochs or duns, round towers which had double walls separated by galleries and staircases. Both are on hill tops. Dun a' Chaolais is above the road as it crosses the neck of the peninsula south of Caolas. The lower courses of the walls of the tower can be seen amidst the rubble of the collapsed higher courses. Dun Bhatarsaigh, on the hilltop west of the township of Vatersay, is even more ruined, its stones having been taken away to be used somewhere else, perhaps in the building of Vatersay House in the eighteenth century. The two brochs may represent the strongholds of the dominant families in North and South Vatersay respectively; the two parts of the islands may still have been separate, or partially separate at that time. Several other small islands in the Barra group, including Sandray, have one broch or dun each, and Barra has several. There appears to be an abandoned broch construction site about 250 metres west of Dun a' Chaolais: part of the wall base of a massive round building was begun but never finished, perhaps because the decision was taken to build Dun a' Chaolais instead. On the south side of North Vatersay, about 200 metres west of the kerbed cairns, is a large mound of huge blocks of stone, grassed over, possibly a much-ruined broch or dun.

Another type of defensive site is on the island of Bioruaslum, off the north-west coast. An arc of walling runs for about 100 metres across the eastern part of the island, the remainder of that part being defended by low sea cliffs and the narrow channel which separates it from the main island. The unusual feature of this site is that the defended area is well *below* the defensive wall, and any attackers would look down on it from the steep hillside. The closest parallels for this site are in Ireland, where they date to the early to middle centuries of the first millennium AD. On a terrace on the south side of the island, outside the defended area, is a group of circular huts of unknown date.

Other sites in Vatersay may be prehistoric. There are a number of boat-shaped stone settings in the Barra Isles of a type which in other islands – Lewis, Colonsay, the Orkney group – have turned out to be Norse burial monuments. Vatersay has about twenty of these, half the total in the islands, and one of them, at Eorasdail, was excavated by the Sheffield archaeologists. Disappointingly, no evidence whatever of their date or function was found; all that could be said was that they were earlier than land boundaries, marked by lines of stones, of the eighteenth or nineteenth centuries. If there had been human bone in them it would not have survived in the acidic soil; but many are a long way inland and up hillsides, and the conclusion was that they were probably not Norse. Other undated occupation levels can be seen in eroding sections of the sandy areas of the island. These are middens and sometimes remains of stone walls. In some cases there are alternating layers of midden and sand, indicating different periods of occupation separated by periods of sand accumulation. There are also ancient soil levels in some sections, indicating periods of stability. Beneath the upper levels of sand of the isthmus, an ancient soil can be seen which had developed on earlier sand dunes, but the dates of these features are unknown. Enclosure walls are being eroded by the sea at Port a' Bhàta, Caolas, and these presumably date from a period when sea level was lower.

Sandray has many prehistoric sites. There are two possible chambered tombs, possible standing stones, and Bronze Age cairns classified as 'bordered' rather than kerbed, where many of the stones enclosing the cairn are upright rather than horizontal. There are several Iron Age round house sites, and a broch or dun high up on the western slopes of Càrn Ghaltair. Archaeologists from Sheffield University excavated part of a mound at Sheader created by the accumulation of successive phases of buildings and occupation debris over 3,500 years. The earliest level is a shell midden dating to about 1500 BC, the Bronze Age, and there were walls and post holes of a later, Iron Age, building. The site was abandoned for a while and reoccupied in medieval times, followed by two phases of eighteenth- to nineteenth-century occupation. Finally, there are the houses of the Sandray raiders built during their sojourn there between 1907 and 1911. A very interesting area of Sandray is inland from the beach at the south-east end, where sand has been shifting for thousands of years. It is known as the 'wineglass' on account of its appearance from the sea. Wind erosion of dunes shows occupation levels between periods of sand accumulation, and shifting sand seems to be revealing old land surfaces with stone-built structures and occu-pation debris – shells, animal bones, pottery and worked stone – on them. The stones and artefacts on the bottom of the main 'blow-out', which is about twenty metres deep, probably origi-nated from higher levels and have worked their way down as the sand under them has been blown away. Dating has shown that these occupation levels are Bronze Age and Iron Age.

Western Scotland was settled by Gaelic speaking 'Scotti' – hence Scotland – from northern Ireland during the first several centuries AD. Their language and culture gradually took over from the native Pictish culture. Nearby Pabbay has one of only two so-called Pictish symbol stones in the Outer Hebrides. These are memorial stones bearing symbols of a design common to this type of monument, and probably date from between the fifth and seventh centuries. Traditionally, the Hebrides were Christianised by St Columba and his followers after his arrival in Iona from Ireland in 563. The Celtic type of Christianity was based on the monastic ideal, and there is evidence for Christians, probably hermits, living in Barra and Pabbay in the following centuries: there are at least three gravestones bearing incised crosses in Pabbay, and an early cross was added to the symbol stone.

The name Pabbay is derived from the Old Norse for Hermits' or Priests' Isle, indicating the inhabitants at the time of the Norse (Viking) raiding and settlement of the Hebrides which began about 795. An Irish monk, Dicuil, said of the Hebrides in about 825, 'Some of these islands are small; nearly all alike are separated by narrow channels, and in them for nearly a hundred years hermits have dwelt, sailing from our Scotia. Now, because of these robbers the Northmen, they are empty of anchorites.' It is possible that there were hermitages on Vatersay and other islands south of Barra, too; they all had chapels in later times, which may have had early origins or been built on the sites of earlier buildings.

Being on the sea route from Norway to Ireland and the Isle of Man, the Hebrides were used as bases for raids further south. According to one of the Norse sagas, Onund Wooden-leg was the first Viking to come to Barra, in 871. He arrived with five ships, drove out a local ruler, Kjarval, and plundered in Scotland and Ireland. 'They went on warfare in the summers, but were in the Barra Isles in the winters.' Graves of these early settlers have been found on Barra, dating from the ninth century, before the Norse adopted Christianity.

In time the Norse raiders became settlers, and the Hebrides became part of the Norse Kingdom of the Isles. The settlement was on such a scale that their language became the predominant one, at least for place-names. The extent of Norse settlement in the Barra Isles is uncertain; it was less dense than in Lewis, and there are relatively few names which indicate actual settlements of Norse speakers. There is Borve in Barra, Sheader in Sandray, and Suinsibost in Mingulay. There is a tradition that a bishop stayed in a house at Treasabhaig in Viking times.[2]

Many of the place-names have Norse elements which survived after Gaelic reasserted itself following the loss of Norse political control in the thirteenth century, and the actual meanings of the names was forgotten. The -ay or -a endings of the names of the islands are Norse, being derived from the word for island, and some of the other elements in the names are also Norse. In some names, the elements have changed so much over time that their origins and meanings are uncertain. The name Vatersay itself is one of these. There are various possible derivations of the first element, all of them Old Norse. One is from veðr, 'weather side', referring to the coastline exposed to the westerly winds. Another is from vaðill, 'ford', referring to the isthmus as a place which boats could be dragged across from one bay to the other. Then there is vatn, 'water', which would refer to sea-water and the long coastline. Sandray, Sanndraigh in Gaelic, derives from the Old Norse for 'island of the sands'.

The place-names are descriptive or refer to the use to which places were put, or to events or to people. Uidh derives from Old

Norse eið, 'isthmus'. Theisheabhal Mòr, the name of a hill, derives from the Old Norse words hestr, 'horse', and fjall, 'mountain'; mòr is Gaelic for 'big'. Some names have both Norse and Gaelic elements. Others are wholly Gaelic and in many cases more recent. Allt a' Mhuilinn, for instance, means 'stream of the mill', indicating that it once powered a water mill; it is one of the streams draining into the north side of Bàgh Siar (West Bay). On the other side of the bay is an inlet of the sea called Sloc Mhartainn. Sloc is Gaelic for 'gully', Mhartainn is Martin. The tradition is that Martin was an Irish itinerant trader who was staying at Vatersay House when his host's brother offered to take him to a ceilidh, but he killed Martin instead and threw him in the gully.[3]

The Norse Kingdom of the Isles reverted to the Scottish crown in 1266 and was thereafter ruled by the Lords of the Isles. The Scottish clans originated in the period between the twelfth and fourteenth centuries, as groups of people who claimed kinship with, and owed allegiance to, a hereditary chief. The clan occupied a particular territory within which all property was held by the chief on behalf of the clan; the clan members paid rent for land in kind and in military service. By 1427, the MacNeils had emerged as the chiefs of Barra, for in that year they were granted the Barra Isles by the Lords of the Isles. However, they had probably been the chiefs for some time; they claimed descent from 'Neil of the Nine Hostages', king of Ireland in the fourth century AD.

Many of the remains of drystone dikes, and circular structures or buildings dotted about the island, probably belong to the medieval and later periods. These structures could have been animal pens, storage huts or shelters. They could even have been shieling huts, built where cattle were taken to graze away from the settlements in the spring and summer, although it is unlikely that the people would have actually lived in the huts since their homes would not have been far away. Another feature of uncertain date is a seaweed-covered arc of stones running across the head of Bàgh Chornaig, exposed at low tide. This was a fish trap, the fish being trapped as the tide fell. There are also traces of fish traps on the north and south sides of the tidal strand linking the small island of Orosaigh to the Caolas peninsula.[4]

So there is abundant evidence of human occupation of Vatersay – or perhaps one should say for the earlier period, the two islands that are now Vatersay – going back at least 5,000 years. Vatersay and the seas around it had a variety of resources for supporting a substantial population, and the sea was a highway rather than the barrier it has become in the last century.

2. Tacksmen, landlords, tenants, 1549–1850

Vatersay was mentioned for the first time by name in about 1549, in *A description of the Western Isles of Scotland* by Donald Munro, High Dean of the Isles. He described 'Wattersay' as 'twa myle in lenthe and ane myle in breadthe, ane excellent Raid [road, i.e. harbour] for shippes that comes ther to fische, ane faire maine ile, inhabit and manurit [cultivated] abounding in corne and gersing [grazing] with goode pasturage for sheep. All thir nine Iles forsaid had a chapel in every Ile. This Ile pertains to the Bishope of the Iles.'

The nine islands mentioned are the five main islands south of Barra and four smaller ones; while there is little doubt that each of the main islands had a chapel, the same cannot be said of the smaller ones. Vatersay's chapel was Cille Bhrianain, (the Chapel of St Brendan) on the tidal island of Uinessan, at the eastern end of the Uidh peninsula. The surviving walls, barely above ground level, measure about eleven by five metres (35 by 16 feet). There is an enclosure around the ruin, labelled on early Ordnance

Survey maps 'graveyard'. There is a tradition that there was another chapel in Vatersay, within the present burial ground adjacent to the township of Vatersay. It was known as Cille Mhoire, the Chapel of St Mary, and the burial ground was once known as St Mary's. There is a slight eminence within it, and other chapels in the islands, such as Cille Bhrianain and the chapels on Pabbay (at least the traditional site of the chapel) and Mingulay, each within a graveyard, are on knolls. According to Nan MacKinnon, there were other cemeteries in former times in Vatersay. The remains of Sandray's chapel, dedicated to St Bride or Bridget, were recorded by the officers of the Ordnance Survey in 1878 and 1901 to the east of Bàgh Bàn on the north-east coast, in a graveyard. In 1915 a sheep fank (enclosure for shearing and dipping sheep) was said to occupy the site. Both chapel and graveyard have entirely disappeared under drifting sand.[1]

It is not known when the chapels in the islands were built, but it could have been in the twelfth century when the Roman diocesan system of church organisation was introduced and the parish of Barra became part of the Diocese of the Isles. The parish church of Barra at Cille Bharra was built at this time, although there may have been an earlier building on the site.

Cille Bhrianain is the traditional burial place of Mor nan Ceann, (Morag of the Heads), wife of one Gilleonan, twenty-ninth chief of the Clan MacNeil in the fifteenth century. There are two versions of the origin of the 'heads'. According to one, the heads were those of cattle: she liked to dine on a fresh ox-tongue every day. This had a drastic effect on MacNeil's herd, and she was eventually persuaded that her passion did not have to be indulged so frequently. In the other version the heads are human: after her husband's death she had his two sons from a previous marriage beheaded so that her son would become chief. The executions took place at Bàgh Chornaig. She also got rid of servants who became too old to work by putting them in 'am priosan', the prison, an arrangement of rocks at Port à Bhàta, Caolas, which filled up at high tide, drowning the occupants. Before she died she expressed the wish to be buried in her native Coll or within sight of it. The day of the conveyance of her body to Coll being foggy, the burial party decided to bury her on Uinessan, and she was interred in a sitting position in the ruined chapel, from which, it was believed, Coll would be visible. When the air cleared it transpired that the island of Muldoanich blocked the view of Coll, which would have been very hard to see at the best of times, being low-lying. In fact, even without Muldoanich, the view of Coll would be blocked by part of Uinessan itself! MacNeil resisted calls for her to be reburied in accordance with her wishes, saying that she had caused enough trouble during life. According to a version of the story, the chapel was built by Mor nan Ceann.[2]

There are various other traditions of the island. The story of the Gold Ship is given in Appendix 3. A writer in 1845 wrote of sea-caves on the west of the island, 'where, of old, cargoes of smuggled commodities were wont to be deposited. It is reported that, somewhere in this island, a large chestful of dollars was once secreted, either by one of the old piratical chieftains or by some smugglers, afterwards prevented from rescuing it; but notwithstanding many eager researches, no one has as yet been fortunate to discover where the subterraneous treasure lies.'[3]

'We have been credibly informed,' wrote Alexander Nicolson, the minister, in 1840, 'by a gentleman of some information, and a native of the place, that he had seen on the island of Watersay, the entire skeleton of a trooper and his horse, where they had fallen side by side on the sand, with some pieces of the armour pretty entire, where the sand-drift had exposed them to view.' Although sand does drift and expose old things and land surfaces to view, it is, as the minister himself said, 'difficult to account for the fact.'[4]

Munro's statement that 'This Ile pertains to the Bishope of the Iles' applied to all the islands south of Barra, giving rise to the term 'Bishop's Isles'. The 'five isles of Barray' are listed in a rental list of 1561, while Martin Martin, writing about 1695, says they were 'held of the bishop' but elsewhere he says that the islands around Barra 'belong in property to MacNeil'. In what sense the islands were the bishop's is unclear, which probably means they were not of great importance.[5]

Church organisation in the islands broke down at the time of the Protestant Reformation, which culminated in 1560 with the legal establishment of the reformed Scottish Kirk. Roman Catholicism survived in some remote places such as the southern Outer Hebrides, and in 1636 an Irish Franciscan, Cornelius Ward, was sent to 'reconcile' or reconvert the people to the old religion. He spent a month working in the Barra Isles and the following year worked 'in the Bishop's Isles where no priest had set foot since the Reformation.' The first priest to do so, Dermot Duggan, arrived in Barra in 1654, where he found 'a people so devout and anxious to learn that I was astonished.' Father Duggan spent five years working in the islands, and had reconciled the people as far north as Benbecula, when he died. This marks the northern limit of Roman Catholicism to this day. A later worker in Barra, Father Francis MacDonnell, complained of the 'danger and difficulty in taking vestments between the five islands where there are Catholics.' There is no mention of chapels in the smaller islands in the accounts of these workers, but in 1700 Bishop Nicolson wrote of Barra that 'there are six other inhabited islands, and there is a chapel in each,' so the chapels had survived the Reformation.[6]

Priests lived in fear of persecution at this time, and held Mass in the open. According to local tradition, a large flat-topped rock near the shore at Beannachan, Vatersay, which means 'blessed place,' was used as an altar or mass-stone in the seventeenth century. A Barra crofter who was asked in 1894 whether there had ever been a church in Vatersay, said he did not know of one, but there was 'a house of congregation'.[7]

According to an account of 1620, the MacNeil, the 'Master or Superior' of the southern islands, received as duty 'half of ther cornes, butter, cheese, and all other commodities which does incres or grow to them in the yeare. And hath ane officer or serjeant in everie Illand to uptake the samen.' Martin Martin, writing about 1695, adds, 'the Steward of the Lesser and Southern Islands is reckoned a great man here, in regard to the Perquisites due to him' by each family, in the form of barley. Martin Martin portrays MacNeil as a paternalistic clan chief who fulfilled his obligations to his tenants and thus ensured their support. Writing of Mingulay and the 'adjacent islands', he says that if a tenant's wife died, 'without which he cannot manage his Affairs, nor beget followers to Mackneil', MacNeil would find a new one for him, and likewise he would find a new husband for a tenant's widow; he would make good the loss of a cow, and also took elderly tenants into his own home and maintained them until their death.[8]

During the eighteenth century Vatersay begins to emerge from its obscurity. By now the island formed a tack, that is, a unit of land leased to a landlord or 'tacksman', often a kinsman of the clan chief, to whom the inhabitants, his tenants, would pay rent. Sandray was also a tack at this time. The MacNeils of Vatersay were descended from Niall Uibhesteach, son and heir of chief Ruairi an Tartair (Roderick the Turbulent), but he was dispossessed in 1615. A descendant, Hector, died before 1703 leaving three young children: a son, Donald, and two daughters. This Donald MacNeil had become a Protestant by 1725 when he encouraged the fiercely anti-Catholic Society for Propagating Christian Knowledge to establish a school in Barra to combat 'popery', as Catholicism was called. He may have converted to Protestantism in order to make himself more eligible to inherit the estate of Barra as nearest Protestant heir of the then chief, who was his first cousin. He would have been unable to do this as a Roman Catholic, an example of the discrimination Catholics suffered. This didn't happen, but he did manage to convert the next chief, Roderick the Gentle (the penultimate chief, and Donald's grandson) to Protestantism. Donald was described by Walker in 1764 as 'a man of excellent Principles and the chief support of the Protestant interest in that part of the World.' Donald's son, Angus, became the Church of Scotland minister of Barra from 1771 to 1774. A later minister of Barra, Edmund MacQueen, wrote in 1794 that he preached every fourth Sunday

at Vatersay – to the MacNeils, that is. The Vatersay MacNeils
were compared favourably with tacksmen elsewhere in the
Hebrides in the 1780s, being 'of too gentle and generous a
disposition to abuse the confidence placed in them by their chief,
by trampling on a poor but kindred people.'[9]

The first population figures for individual islands are recorded
in 1764 by Walker: Vatersay had 104 people and Sandray, 40.
The rent for Vatersay was £35; for Sandray £12. At this time the
arable land was held in common by the tenants, who rotated
among themselves the patches of land they cultivated, a system
known as 'runrig'. Individual holdings or crofts developed later.
The Vatersay tenants were living in various places: remains of
houses – some of them visible only as shallow hollows in the turf
– dating from before the eviction of the people in 1850 can be
seen in coastal locations around the island, such as on the Uidh
peninsula, in the Caolas area, at Tresabhaigh and at Eorasdail.
There would also have been houses on the site of the township of
Vatersay. The houses, so-called 'black houses', were of the Barra
Isles type: rectangular with rounded external corners and a
central door in one of the long walls. The walls were about
1.5 metres (5 feet) thick, faced inside and out with stone, the gap
filled with earth and stones. Turf was also used as a building
material. The walls were built to the same height all round, 1.5 to
2 metres, and the rounded thatched roof rested on the inside
edge of the walls, so that there were no eaves for the wind to get
a grip of, but it meant that the rain drained directly into the walls.
Small houses of this type can be seen in Sandray, which was
cleared of its inhabitants in 1835. Until the later nineteenth
century there were no windows as such, only openings in the

thatch, and no fireplaces or chimneys, the fire being in the centre of the floor. Houses of this type were referred to in Vatersay in 1853. Some of the nineteenth-century visitors to Barra were horrified by the standard of housing, but in one respect it was in advance of the islands to the north: the houses generally accommodated humans only, the cattle living in byres.[10]

Many of the stone or stone-and-earth dikes on the island belong to the pre-1850 clearance period, when boundaries were being laid out in association with the introduction of crofts, while others are pre-crofting. There are also boundary dikes between townships. A massive earth bank crossing the south-eastern arm of the island from Beinn Chuidhir southwards was described by Neil MacPhee in 1910 as 'the old dike which was for generations the march between the two townships.' However, its scale makes it no ordinary boundary, and it may originate in a much earlier period.[11]

The people would have raised black cattle – the islands' most valuable export – and sheep. They fished for cod and ling, some of which they dried and took in their small open boats to Glasgow and northern Ireland to sell. They grew barley, oats and, from 1762, potatoes. Potatoes could be grown in poorer soil than grain, and on such soil they were planted in so-called 'lazy beds'. These were ridges created by digging shallow parallel drainage ditches up to 2 metres apart, laying the soil on the intervening strips, then adding manure and seaweed. Lazy beds were created for potatoes, so are no earlier than the later eighteenth century; they cover large areas of Vatersay. Yields were high, and this meant that the islands could support a higher population.[12]

In 1794 MacQueen wrote that Vatersay was 'divided into two distinct farms, one, possessed by Mr McNeil of Watersay, the other is now in the hands of the proprietor [Roderick the Gentle], called the farm of Kilis' (Caolas). The Vatersay Mac-Neils' farm was the southern part of the island, centred on Vatersay House. Maps indicate that the Caolas farm buildings were on the machair, at the west end of Caolas beyond the end of the present tarred road. They may be the two buildings marked as ruins on the Ordnance Survey map of 1880 and traceable in the turf in the potato ground there. The map also marks a lime kiln near these buildings, which would have been used to burn shells for lime which was then spread on the poorer soils to improve the grazing. By the time the next edition of the map was surveyed in 1901 the kiln had gone out of use and a blackhouse had been built by the Ferguson family on or next to the site, using its stones. The farms would have been used mainly for raising black cattle. No population figure is given in 1794, unlike for the other southern islands which were inhabited by tenant families, suggesting that the status of the Vatersay people was different. The registers of baptisms and marriages of the parish church of Barra at Craigston, which begin in 1805, name only two centres of population, Vatersay – where the township of Vatersay is now – and Kyles (Caolas). Vatersay had the larger population as there were more children being baptised there. Sandray had nine families in 1794.[13]

Vatersay House was built sometime in the later eighteenth century. According to local tradition it was built by one of the MacNeils of Vatersay for his two sisters. This could have been Donald, who was still living in 1764. It is a modest building, in contrast to Eoligarry House which was built by Roderick the Gentle after his marriage in 1788. The MacNeils of Barra had left Kisimul Castle, Castlebay, early in the century and had subsequently lived at Vaslan.

There were dramatic changes in the Highlands and Islands in the later eighteenth and nineteenth centuries. The old clan system began to crumble, particularly as a result of the repressive measures following the failure of the Jacobite uprising of 1745. The clan chiefs, deprived of their traditional status and role, and increasingly leading expensive lifestyles in Edinburgh and London, needed regular cash income. They achieved this by establishing commercial ventures such as sheep farming, fishing and kelping. This was the gathering and burning of seaweed to create an alkaline ash for use in the soap and glass industries, and its development was to have far-reaching consequences. Chiefs forced their tenants to work at kelping by dividing up the arable land, which had been held in common by the tenants, into individual plots called crofts, their tenants being called crofters. The crofts were deliberately kept too small to provide a living for a family, and rents were raised, forcing the crofters to work for cash in the kelping industry, which was a condition of their tenancy. Kelping was introduced to Barra in 1763, and an oven used to burn the kelp has been identified at Traigh Bharlais, Vatersay. According to tradition there was another at Port a' Bhàta, Caolas (see Appendix 4). The crofting system had begun to be introduced into Barra by about 1815, and the process was still going on in the 1820s.[14]

Clan chiefs also began the process which became known as the Clearances, evicting tenants from fertile land to turn it into more profitable grazing for sheep. Roderick the Gentle evicted people from Eoligarry, Barra, to create his farm in the late eighteenth century. Clearances gathered pace after the 1820s when the market for kelp collapsed and tenants could no longer pay their rents. Some people opted to seek better lives by emigrating, but for others it was not voluntary; emigration was used by some landlords to get rid of a redundant population. Emigration from Barra to Canada – mainly Cape Breton, Nova Scotia – had begun in 1772. Vatersay people are known to have emigrated in 1817 (and before), 1821 and 1826, and people from Bàgh na Greot in Sandray emigrated in 1802. The peninsula of Iona, in the Bras d'Or Lake, Cape Breton, was originally named Sandray by settlers from there. Eventually, clan chiefs were forced to sell up altogether, and their ancestral lands were bought by commercial landlords.[15]

The penultimate MacNeil of Barra, Roderick the Gentle, who ruled from 1763 to 1822, was, on the whole, a paternalistic chief of the old school. However, he increased the tenants' rents hugely, by up to 600% in Barra. The rent for Vatersay rose only modestly, from £35 in 1764 to £60 in 1810, presumably because the tacksmen were his relatives; that of Sandray rose from £12 to £42. None of the four southernmost isles have large quantities of kelp, so it is hard to see how the tenants were expected to pay for such rises. It was not by dividing up holdings and settling more people there, as was the case in Barra. There were nine tenants in Sandray in 1810, as there had been in 1794.[16]

By 1810 a rental list names four tenants at Caolas, but the farm there is also mentioned. The surnames represented in Caolas in the early years were MacNeil, MacLean, MacSwan, Campbell; in later years MacIntyre, MacInnes, Gillies appear. In the settlement near Vatersay Farm there was MacNeil, MacLean, MacKenzie, MacMillan, MacIntyre, MacDonald. A map of 1823 shows buildings at Vatersay Farm, at Caolas (on the machair), and at Uidh, roughly where the church is now, and at Port Deas, the southern beach at Caraigrigh. The various settlements in Sandray are not named separately. The church registers record many marriages in which the partners were from different islands, so there were family ties between all the island communities.[17]

Further glimpses are provided by an account book kept from 1818 to 1822 by the priest, Rev. Angus McDonald of Barra, who seems to have kept accounts for people in all the islands. People in Caolas and Vatersay are mentioned, including Mr Hugh MacNeil, Caolas, possibly the farmer there; he was son of Donald, tacksman of Vatersay. 'Mrs MacNeil' is also mentioned. People owed an annual fee for seats in the church at Craigston, Barra. Some of the Vatersay people appear to have been selling barley. Nearly all the entries for Sandray people concern fishing. The catch included lobsters and basking sharks, which were caught for their liver oil. These huge harmless creatures swim close to the surface in the summer and would have been easy targets with harpoons. Five Sandray men and one from Mingulay were involved. The catching of these sharks was mentioned in 1794, but by 1840 they were no longer caught because the fishermen did not have the necessary equipment.[18]

A visitor to Vatersay in 1816, the geologist John MacCulloch, wrote an amusing – if patronising – account of his experience of

Vatersay, referring to his host as the tenant and laird, thus Donald MacNeil.

I had here an opportunity of imagining how life is passed in a remote island, without society or neighbours, and where people are born and die without ever troubling themselves to enquire whether the world contains any other countries than Vatersa and Barra. The amusement of the evening consisted in catching scallops for supper, milking the cows, and chasing rabbits; and this I presume is pretty nearly the usual round of occupation. The whole group of the south-ern islands is seen here from the southern part of the island . . . we were promised a boat in the morning to visit all these islands, and I therefore went to bed full of hope. I had forgotten that I was in a Highland land.

Morning came, and six, but breakfast did not come till ten. Then came the cows to be milked and the calves to be admired; for in these countries of blatant cattle, a calf is a much more important object than a child, and its nursing an affair of the purest affection. At length we arrived at the beach, and then the laird recollected that, a few days before, his boat had been carried away by the tide and dashed in pieces; as he had forgotten to anchor or fasten her. But there was another boat on the island; we should probably find it; which we accordingly did. With unusual foresight he had borrowed some oars the preceding evening; but they had been left on the beach within high water mark, and had floated off in search of the original boat. There were oars to be borrowed somewhere: they would be ready

at twelve, or one, or two o'clock . . . we then however
discovered that there were no men; our kind host having
sent all his people to Barra . . . another messenger was
despatched to borrow four of the islanders. The borrowed
oars of one fisherman were at length fitted to the borrowed
boat of another: but when the second messenger returned,
all the islanders were absent making kelp.

Donald MacNeil was reported to have made a 'park' or
enclosure for agricultural purposes in 1819, according to Roderick
the Gentle writing to Angus MacDonald, priest of Barra. Two
years later MacNeil wrote: 'I am much pleas'd that Watersay reaps
so much benefit from his park, and I hope your example, and Mr
Nicleson's [the minister], and his will at last have influence, and
make the tenants wish to have a small spot they can call their own.'
This presumably refers to the introduction of individually held
crofts. It is possible that this park is the square enclosure which
appears on the maps of 1880 and 1904 and which still exists on the
machair on the northern edge of the township of Vatersay.[19]

The Sandray people were privileged to get a school in 1822.
The teacher was sent by the Gaelic Schools Society, which had
been set up in 1811 with the aim of teaching people in remote
areas to read the Bible in Gaelic. Barra had various such schools
between 1818 and 1825. The minister of Barra, Alexander
Nicolson, wrote in June 1822:

I have likewise to draw the attention of the Society to the
destitute situation of the island of Sandra* in this parish. It is
inhabited by several families, who have never as yet had the

opportunity of acquiring the least degree of knowledge. They are all Roman Catholics, and as far as I know have not a single Bible amongst them. I have spoke to the people about the prospect they had of a School from your Society, and they seemed highly delighted at the idea of their children being soon able to read. They promised to have a comfortable house provided for the Teacher's reception, and that the number of scholars would amount to from twenty-five to thirty. One man said he would send eight of his own family to school.

* A Gaelic teacher has been appointed to Sandra; the school was opened in November last, and was then attended by twenty-two males and ten females. [This was added the following year] [20]

Roderick MacNeil (the Gentle) died in 1822 and was succeeded by his son, also Roderick, and known as General MacNeil. Roderick senior had left massive debts, which his son attempted to pay off by adopting a much more commercial – and tyrannical – policy towards his estate. He began the process of clearing crofters from the fertile west coast of Barra to make way for more profitable sheep, and established Castlebay as a fishing village, for the processing of cod and ling. He threatened to evict fishermen from their holdings if they sold their fish in Glasgow or to passing vessels, rather than in Castlebay so that he would get his cut.[21] He wrote to the priest of Barra in 1825, 'You will do well to advise your friends at Sandra, and all the Leaders as they are termed, to mind well what they are about, if they wish to remain at Barra. They are of little or no importance to me, whatever may be their value to you, and if I don't on my arrival find them heart and hand engaged in fishing, *I pledge you my honour* they shall tramp, and the land shall be this ensuing spring occupied by *strangers.*'[22] Whether he carried out this threat in Sandray is not known, but he certainly did in Barra, and imported 'strangers', all Protestants, mainly from North Uist and Tiree.

The Sandray people, who were all evicted in 1835, lived at various locations around the coast, mainly at Sheader on the west, Bàgh Bàn on the east, and Bàgh na Greot on the south. Remains of houses can be seen at Bàgh na Greot and at a few other locations, and represent early forms of the house types of the Barra Isles described above. They are very small compared to later nineteenth-century houses, up to about 7 metres (22 feet) in length. At Sheader, the stones of the houses were used by the Sandray raiders to build their houses in 1907–1908, and one of these buildings was excavated by Sheffield University archae-ologists in 1995. Under the floor of a raider house they found the floor and hearth of a pre-1835 house, and a halfpenny dating to 1776 or 1796. Any buildings near the site of the chapel at Bàgh Bàn were probably also demolished or modified by the shepherds who lived there after 1835, or were buried under sand. Sherds of pottery and other artefacts of eighteenth-century date in an area of shifting sand roughly half way between there and the beach to the south indicate that people were also living in that area. Apart from the two later settlements and, no doubt, some animal pens and enclosures built by the shepherds, Sandray's cultural land-scape of settlements and field systems is unique in the Barra Isles in that it has hardly been modified since the clearance of 1835.[23]

In 1825 General MacNeil also took back the farm of Vatersay which had been in the hands of MacNeil tacksmen for 200 years. Hugh MacNeil, eldest son of the last tacksman, Donald, wrote in 1827, 'our family has left their native home being forced from the place by that monster of ingratitude the Colonel' (as he then was). The family lived in the Isle of Man for a few years. The General seems to have had a change of heart, because after Donald died in 1830 his widow, Margaret – who was the General's aunt – was allowed to stay 'in possession of house, garden, and park, with grass of 8 cows, 2 horses, and a few sheep, rent free.' She was still in occupation in 1837. By 1831 Hugh had established a shop in Castlebay, and had taken on the tenancies of the public houses in Barra.[24]

It is possible that crofters were also evicted when the MacNeils were dispossessed, because there is a curious absence of baptisms or marriages of anybody from Vatersay from the church records between 1827 and 1831. Three families from the township of Gortein, on the Bentangaval peninsula, settled at Uidh, Vatersay, in about 1832, when people are first recorded there; Gortein was deserted by 1835. By 1836 these Gortein people had moved on, and all the tenants of Uidh were evictees from Sandray. They, in turn, were evicted in 1838, and some of them ended up in Mingulay, along with people evicted from other places. They swelled the population of Mingulay, which had implications for the island and for Vatersay many decades later. Possible evidence of the clearance of Vatersay is the record that MacNeil's men seized sheep from a Kentangaval crofter and took them to Vatersay in about 1827. The crofter protested and she was evicted. MacNeil's men were also ordered to seize cattle from every crofter in Barra, and on one occasion to kill all the crofters' sheep.[25]

According to Murdoch MacKinnon of Barra, who gave evidence to the 'Deer Forest Commission' in Barra in 1894, there were thirty families in Vatersay sixty years before, paying £30 rent annually, and he mentioned Roderick the Gentle's sister living there. He also said the people of Vatersay were evicted 'eight times' towards the end of General MacNeil's time. Evidence for such evictions can be found in the church registers, as we have seen, although absence of records does not necessarily imply absence of people.[26]

MacNeil's most ambitious, but ultimately disastrous, attempt to raise revenue was to build a factory for reprocessing kelp. In theory the end product or 'enhanced kelp' would sell for a higher price than the product of the first stage in the process, thus making the venture worthwhile. The factory was at Northbay, Barra, and there are indications that MacNeil forced tenants to work there between 1833 and 1837. One of the buildings was called the 'barracks' and may have accommodated these labourers. The significance for the islands south of Barra is the report that the inhabitants of all of them were evicted by MacNeil to make way for sheep in 1835 'so that for a time there was not an inhabitant within 13 miles of the lighthouse' – of Barra Head, Berneray – a distance which includes Vatersay. This suggests that for some of the islands the clearance was short-lived, but the people of Berneray, who had been evicted the previous year, are said to have worked at the kelp factory, no doubt against their will, until 1837. This was about the time it ceased production, having been partly responsible for MacNeil's bankruptcy and the sequestration of the estate; and a creditor, John Gordon, also demanded that money he had loaned MacNeil be repaid. Inhabitants of other islands may also have worked there. Sandray was cleared permanently, as we have seen, and was added to Vatersay Farm for grazing, as was Bentangaval, the southern part of Barra adjacent to Vatersay.[27]

The rent for Vatersay and Caolas (farms) had rocketed to £550 by 1836 (in 1810 the rent for Vatersay had been £60). However, the farm was still in the possession of General MacNeil himself, because when in that year an auditor attempted to go to Vatersay to make an inventory of the stock, he was told that the previous day 200 cattle had been taken to Barra and let loose. General MacNeil was bankrupt, and was trying to hide or sell his moveable property before it was seized and sold on behalf of creditors. The estate of Barra was put up for sale in 1837, after many centuries of ownership by the Clan MacNeil.[28]

The 1820s and 1830s were therefore a time of turmoil, poverty and suffering in the islands, with people being evicted from place to place, and having their cattle and sheep seized or even killed. Among the new Protestants being imported was Duncan Sinclair from Appin in Argyll who was employed as a shepherd by General MacNeil in Vatersay (previously he had been a gardener at Eoligarry House), an example of a Protestant outsider being employed in preference to a local Catholic. He married Mary MacNeil, a Catholic from Mingulay, in 1833, and their first child, Donald, was born and baptised in Vatersay only three months later. They were still in Vatersay two years later when their son, John, was baptised, and ten years after that they were living in Berneray where they remained. John later moved to Mingulay and returned to Vatersay in old age at the time of the raids. Although the children were baptised by the Catholic priest at the behest of their mother, their father had them baptised by the Church of Scotland minister as well.[29]

The Barra estate was bought in 1840 by the above-mentioned Colonel John Gordon of Cluny, Aberdeenshire, who also bought South Uist and Benbecula. He had large estates in five counties and was noted for implementing the improvements in agriculture of the time. He had ambitions for Barra in this regard, but it is not clear exactly what he had in mind. It was said that he did not visit his property at all during his eighteen-year tenure – he was the ultimate absentee landlord – although he had visited it before he bought it. He also offered the island to the government as a penal colony, so he was quite ready to get rid of every single inhabitant. He was said to be the richest commoner in Scotland, and was buying property purely as an investment, like most of the new owners of former clan lands. He was, however, one of the worst. Between 1846 and 1851, when the failure of the potato crop due to blight caused famine in the Highlands and Islands (as in Ireland), he became notorious for his meanness in providing relief in the form of grain, to use as payment for people working on public works such as roads. Gordon continued his predecessors' policy of evicting tenants to create sheep farms and encouraging, or forcing, emigration to Canada. Voluntary emigration was no bad thing, as Barra could not support its population, but Gordon became notorious also for the brutality with which his men – encouraged by the minister of the Church of Scotland, Henry Beatson – forced people onto emigration ships and hunted down anyone who tried to escape. Contemporary descriptions are akin to accounts of slave-catching on the coast of west Africa. About 450 Barra tenants were shipped off to Montreal and Quebec in 1850 and 1851, with no provision being made for them at the other end.[30]

By the time of the population census of 1841 an Alexander Cameron was the farming tenant. His wife and two young children, and possibly other relatives, are also recorded living with him. There were fifteen other families on the island, fishermen, crofters and cottars – people who had no land of their own, often the children of crofters – giving a total population of eighty-four. The population was not constant, however. Few of the families are the same as those recorded in the church registers before then and afterwards, up to the final eviction of 1850. Sandray was inhabited in 1841 only by a shepherd and an agricultural labourer and their families. They lived east of the beach at Bàgh Bàn, near the site of the medieval chapel and graveyard.

The last evictions from Vatersay were part of a policy implemented by Colonel Gordon throughout his estate to get rid of crofting tenants from fertile land and let it to commercial farmers as grazing, for much higher rent. An observer reported of Barra in 1851: 'There have been many changes from crofts to grazings of late.' Almost the entire population of crofters and fishermen were cleared from Vatersay in 1850 or 1851. The child of a Vatersay crofting family was baptised in August 1850, but by the time of the population census in April 1851, nearly all the crofters and fishermen had gone. Neil MacPhee, writing in 1909, referred to the evictions in three letters; in two, he said they had taken place fifty-eight years before, and in another, sixty.[31]

Most of the Vatersay evictees ended up in Barra, but a few went to the mainland and to Mull, and one family emigrated to Canada on the *Admiral* in 1851. The descendants of those evicted never gave up their claim to Vatersay. As the raiders said in 1907, they continued to bury their dead in Vatersay. This is confirmed by the civil registers of deaths, which between 1855 and 1860 record place of burial as well as place of death: only three of the fourteen people who were buried in Vatersay (in St Mary's cemetery, which is still in use) had died there, the remainder died in Barra, most of them in the Castlebay area.[32]

Thus ended a long period of habitation by local people. The first three centuries of Vatersay's recorded history saw the MacNeils of Vatersay, relatives of the MacNeils of Barra, take on the tack, or farm, of Vatersay. The island continued to be inhabited by tenants, who became crofters when that system was introduced to the islands in the early nineteenth century. As in the other islands, the people were involved in the kelping industry and there had been emigration to Canada. For more than twenty years before the final eviction of crofters from Vatersay in 1850, the inhabitants suffered from the tyrannical policies of the last MacNeil of Barra and his successor, John Gordon. They were evicted from place to place within the island, and evictees from Barra and Sandray were also settled on Vatersay.

3. Farm and shipwreck, 1850–1900

The year 1850 saw the start of a new era for Vatersay. The crofters and fishermen, of whom there had been seventy-six in 1841, were evicted and the whole island (2,338 acres, plus 1,178 acres on Sandray, Flodday, Biruaslum and smaller islands used for grazing) was given over to the farm, based at Vatersay House. The population census taken in April 1851 records the new regime. Top of the list of sixty-four people was the farmer, Donald MacLellan, aged 29, from the island of Taransay, off Harris. Living with him in Vatersay House were sixteen employees, including two dike builders, a quarrier, a mason, a builder, four farm labourers, a dairy maid and a stable boy, as well as domestic staff. In two separate houses were two farm grieves (managers), two further agricultural labourers, and a cow herd. The grieves, mason, builder, cow herd and two labourers were born outside Barra (the Uists, Harris, Skye, and Ross-shire); the remainder were born in Barra parish, including two families of fishermen who had been in Vatersay in 1841, and an agricultural

labourer who had been a crofter in 1841. In all, twelve out of
thirty-six adults in the census were born outside the parish. All
the children were born in Barra parish, indicating that the
incoming families had lived there for some time.

A lot of building work must have been going on at this time.
The dikes are probably the substantial though largely grass-
grown dikes still visible in many places, dividing the machair
from the hill grazings; they are distinguishable from earlier dikes
by their scale. This period of dike-building was probably the last,
because by the time new boundaries for the crofting settlement
were laid out more than fifty years later, wire fencing was being
used. The farm steading – barns, byres and stables forming a
rough square at the bottom of the slope on which Vatersay
House stands – may have been built or added to. The extension
to the north end of the back of Vatersay House may have been
built at this time. Many of the workers had left Vatersay by the
time of the *Annie Jane* shipwreck in September 1853, when there
were said to be only seven or eight men on the island (there were
twenty-three in 1851). By 1861, the population had halved to
thirty-two, nearly all of them incomers.

The farm was used mainly for grazing for cattle, on the
machair, and for sheep, on the hill grazing. Sandray, and, until
1883, the Bentangaval peninsula of Barra, were also used as
grazing by the farm. Horses and pigs were also kept. Hay and
fodder crops such as oats were grown in the area around the farm
and southwards, the area now occupied by the crofts of Vatersay
Township.[1]

On 28 September 1853 an event occurred which catapulted
Vatersay into the headlines, such as they were in those days.

Under the banner 'Appalling shipwreck on the coast of Barra', *The Glasgow Herald* of Monday, 10 October, broke the news thus: 'It is our painful task to announce one of the most mournful shipwrecks which has ever occurred on the coast of Scotland, in connection with which, as we learn from some of the survivors who reached Glasgow on Saturday morning, nearly 400 human beings have perished.'

The *Annie Jane*, carrying emigrants and cargo from Liverpool to Quebec, was wrecked in Bàgh Siar, the west bay of Vatersay. She was a three-masted wooden sailing ship of 1,294 tons, 179 feet long, built in Quebec a few months earlier and on the return voyage to her home port. She was carrying 800 tons of iron in bar, pig and sheet form, and in the form of lengths of railway track for the expanding Canadian network. She also had 300 tons of rope, sails, tea, paper and soap. About 100 of the passengers were blacksmiths and carpenters from Glasgow contracted to work on the expanding railways in Canada, and some of these had brought their families with them. There were 385 adult emigrants from Scotland, Ireland and England, and an unknown number of children, and all were voluntary emigrants, not the victims of enforced emigration by landlords. The forty-one crew brought the total to nearly 500, it was estimated. She sailed on 25 August, but had to turn back after two days because of losing her topmasts in a gale. Some of the passengers left the ship at this point, fearing for their lives. Three days after setting out again she met another gale and suffered damage, but Captain Mason refused to put back for repairs, and threatened to shoot anyone who attempted to take charge of the ship. He eventually agreed to make for Londonderry, but following further storms in which more masts and sails were lost, she became uncontrollable, and for a week drifted helplessly to a point about 300 kilometres (200 miles) beyond the outlying St Kilda. The wind changed to the north and the crew managed to turn her back towards Ireland. The lighthouse of Barra Head (Berneray) was eventually sighted in the distance to the south, and it was hoped that she would drift past the islands out of danger, but on 28 September a westerly storm tore away the remaining sails and drove her inexorably towards destruction on Vatersay. Despite the storm and the darkness, Mason managed to steer the ship clear of the rocks on the north side of Bàgh Siar (had she struck them, nobody would have survived) and towards the beach, in the hope that some lives might be saved.

The *Annie Jane* grounded just before midnight, half a mile from the beach, according to one witness. When the ship struck, *The Glasgow Herald* reported:

The officers and crew were on deck at this fearful con-juncture, and there were also on deck a large number of male passengers who with feelings of despair contemplated their fate, as indicated by the dull outline of the land and the roaring of the surf on the beach. Meanwhile the great majority of the passengers were below in their berths, but the striking of the ship gave them a fearful awakening. Many rushed on deck in a state of nakedness . . . After the first shock was over, the passengers rushed to the boats . . . but as happens too commonly in such melancholy cases, the boats were of no earthly use, for they were all fixed down or secured, or lay bottom up. While the passengers were thus clustered round the boats the ship was struck by a sea of frightful potency, which instantly carried away the dense mass of human beings into the watery waste, and boats and bulwarks went along with them. While this fearful scene was going on upon deck the great majority of the women and children, as well as some of the male passengers, remained below . . . but their time also had come. Another dreadful sea broke on board, and literally crushed part of the deck upon the berths below, which were occupied by terror-stricken women and sleeping children. They were killed rather than drowned, as was fully evidenced by the naked, mutilated and gashed bodies which were afterwards cast on shore . . . the ship broke into three pieces . . . The most of the remaining passengers and seamen now took refuge on the poop, with the exception of seven men, who secured themselves on the topgallant forecastle. The poop fortunately floated well, and was drifted inwards by the wind and each heave of the sea, when it finally grounded about four o'clock. The forecastle came ashore about the same time.

The wreck had been observed from the island almost as soon as day broke, and seven or eight of the Barra men (all who were in the neighbourhood at the time) came down to render such aid as might be in their power. The remains of the mizenmast were still attached to the wreck of the poop, and by the help of the islanders it was placed so as to form a sort of bridge between the poop and shallow water. [According to another report, the islanders brought high-wheeled carts to assist the women in getting ashore.]

When mustered, the number of survivors was found to be 102, of whom one was a child, twelve were women, and twenty-eight belonged to the crew, exclusive of the captain, who was also saved. But the departed friends of the survivors were ashore before them, for the beach was literally lined by their dead bodies . . .

Soon after reaching the shore the survivors repaired to a farm steading, or cluster of houses, which was not far from the beach, and repaired their exhausted energies by rest. The women and officers occupied the houses, and the seamen and male steerage passengers lay down in byre, barn and stable. There was no scarcity of provisions, for some barrels of beef and pork had been washed ashore, and the Barra people supplied potatoes.

Captain Mason, in a letter to the ship's owner, quoted in *The Glasgow Herald*, said that 'the islanders are saving all that they can, and have been very kind to all of us.'

This was a first report of the disaster, based on the accounts of the first group of survivors who left Vatersay four days later, and arrived in Glasgow five days after that. There were many more newspaper accounts over the following weeks, and also an official enquiry and report. The references to Barra rather than Vatersay in the early reports indicate that it was not realised that 'Vatersay Bay', as it was called, was on a separate island.

Within a short time there were reports that the survivors had not been treated as well as at first stated. *The Glasgow Herald* of 24 October 1853 reported: 'We regret to learn that the survivors of the *Annie Jane* are unanimous in stating that they were most shabbily treated by the natives. No efforts were made to administer to their comfort in any way and no food of even the meanest kind was vouchsafed to them. Their clothes and any little articles the survivors could save from the wreck were pitilessly taken away, so that they were left destitute . . . one of the farm servants, in his anxiety for the safety of the porkers, telling some of those who occupied a piggery to mind the pigs.'

At the enquiry, evidence from several survivors was recorded, and many of these accounts give insights into the island and its people at the time, as well as sometimes contradicting each other and other accounts. The following witnesses were accommodated at Vatersay House; Donald MacLellan was away from home at first, and his brother (probably Roderick, of Northbay Farm, Barra) was in charge.

Thomas More, ship's carpenter:

Were you well treated there? – I had many a hungry belly when I was there, and for sixteen days and nights I was never in a bed, and never had my clothes off.

How many houses in the bay where you were wrecked? – A little distance off there were a few of those small turf huts. There were some people lived in them, but they were queer people.

When Mr McLellan came back, he treated you kindly himself? – I hope I shall never more have such like treatment. We had to go on the beach and see if we could find a bit of salt beef, or anything that was washed up from the ship, and they ran away with everything we had belonging to us.

Your clothes? – Yes, every rag.

Who were they? – The islanders, the people working at the wreck.

Where did they come from? – I do not know.

They did not live on that island? – No, they came from a neighbouring island. I think there were only about eight men on that island.

They came from an island to the north, from Uist? – I do not know what they call the place.

William Moore, sail maker:

How did the inhabitants treat you on the island? – Very indifferently indeed. First go off, we got a drink of milk, but the longer we stopped there, the worse we were treated.

John Morgan, passenger:

What did you get to eat when you landed? – We had some barley bread and herrings, and then we had some mutton the following day, and plenty of potatoes.

Where did the others go? – They were down in some cottages that they had on the farm.

What cottages? – Some cottages built up with stones and thatched, and a fire in the middle of the floor.

Charles Brown, seaman:

Did the natives treat you kindly? – They would have treated us very kindly only I do not know whether they had anything to give us. The first they gave us was well enough but the next day they would not give us anything, and we had to go down to the beach and pick up our own salt meat and cook it. The people treated us very well, the governor of the island told us when we got on shore to go down to the other house and we should have plenty of potatoes and herrings. They gave us about a pint of milk then we had some potatoes. Two days after that we got potatoes once more.

The burying of the dead began almost immediately. *The Glasgow Herald* of 10 October reported that: 'The tenant of the island, Mr M'Lellan, was from home but Mr M'Gillivray from Barra was soon on the spot, who took charge, and saw to the decent interment of the bodies. Christian sepulture was deemed impracticable, for the churchyard was ten miles distant. Capacious pits were dug close to the lonely shore, and the poor sufferers were deposited therein.'

The churchyard was that of the Church of Scotland at Cuier, Barra; but the writer did not mention that some of the dead, such as the Irish, would have been Roman Catholics. William MacGillivray was a doctor and farmer at Eoligarry, Barra, and was married to MacLellan's sister; both families were Protestants from Harris. Another witness said that MacLellan's brother supervised the burial of bodies.[2]

Thomas Gray, Chief Clerk of the Wreck Department of the Board of Trade in London, visited Barra in 1866, and wrote a damning report about the treatment of wrecks and other matters. He was told about the plundering of the *Annie Jane* survivors' possessions, and '. . . learnt that the burial was not at all what we would call Christian Burial but two large holes were dug and the people stowed in them, Mr Beatson said "like herrings in a barrel." There is no mark not even a rail or bit of wood to show where these bodies are buried. I should like to see a stone erected . . . The funeral service was a farce and the whole thing brutal and degrading to a degree.'[3]

Mr Beatson was the Church of Scotland minister in Barra.

Gray's wish 'to see a stone erected' was fulfilled in 1881, when the present granite memorial on the dunes above the beach was put up. There is no clue on it as to whose initiative this was, but a visitor in 1887 informs us that, 'A few years ago Robert Macfie, Esq, of Airds and Oban was cruising among the western islands in his yacht', and, on hearing about the disaster, resolved to commemorate it. He commissioned the memorial from a firm of masons who were working in Barra at the time, Cruickshank of Glasgow. The monument is the only listed structure in Vatersay. The inscription states that 'about 350 men, women and children were drowned, and their bodies interred here.' No doubt some of the dead were interred there, but not all of them. The contemporary newspaper reports talk of pits, and Gray specifies two. A map surveyed in 1861–63 marks very precisely a spot nearly 400 metres north-west of there, at the northern end of the beach (and just to the south-east of the ruins of houses at Treasabhaig), with a subdivided rectangle, and the words 'graves of 280 wrecked emigrants'. The spot is a gently sloping terrace in a steep hillside and in that respect looks a likely place; but it is rather high above the sea, and the bodies would have had to have been dragged up rocks and a low cliff in the boulder clay, which the map shows was much the same then as it is today. The soil does not look deep enough to have accommodated a 'capacious pit', but the precision of the location and numbers given cannot be dismissed. On the first edition of the Ordnance Survey map, surveyed in 1878, the words 'Graves of 280 Shipwrecked Emigrants' are strung out along the coast from Treasabhaig southwards suggesting that the surveyors had the older map with them but were not sure about the site. So the exact whereabouts of the victims remains uncertain, as does the number of dead, since the number of live passengers was never recorded.[4]

Gray wrote that the people of Barra

look upon wreck as a common right and do not fail to appropriate what they can. The highest class, the tenant farmers, are but little better than the poorest class in their dealings with wreck. It is true that they proceed in a more indirect manner, but they work towards the one end of making the most they can. After the wreck of the 'Annie Jane' several of the farmers had great quantities of jewellery, one, a magistrate, sent a quantity to Glasgow to be remade. The rumour is that it was appropriated by the MacLellans and MacGillivray. I told him [MacGillivray] I had pretty good evidence where some of the jewellery went to. He turned very white and it was some time before he gained his self possession. It was this gentleman who managed the business of his brother-in-law on whose farm the wreck took place and a bill was sent in to the owners that could only be equalled in fiction. Amongst other things equally monstrous was a charge of £364 for cattle scared so that they would not feed, another for drying ropes in the sands and frightening cows £360 and another for cows that slipped their calves £420 so that it would appear that all the cattle in the island went to see the wreck and that all these cows were in the family way and all in such a precarious state at one and the same time, that the wreck had such an effect on them as to bring on a premature delivery and to cause the offspring to die. This would not be believed in a novel.

Also claimed for were the following: 'burying the dead', £225; 'damage to house', £20; 'fifteen days board and lodging for sixty-eight people', £120; 'circuitous route which had to be taken for seaweed', £127, referring to the hardships faced by MacLellan's workers in being obliged to make a detour round the wreck to reach the seaweed which was needed for fertiliser. The total claimed was £1,736. The bill was contested, and the court awarded £156, mainly for accommodation and burials.

Mr Beatson, the minister, informed Gray that:

> One of the MacLellans went to Skye and was giving away a quantity of jewellery. He says that it is well known in Barra, but that everyone would deny it for the credit of the place, that MacGillivray had property from the 'Annie Jane'. Mr Beatson gave information to the relatives of the dead which led to their asking some disagreeable questions about their property that had been appropriated by the inhabitants and some of the magistrates, and for this he had his cattle harried and killed; and to save himself from utter ruin the remainder were sold under the value to a magistrate, who it was afterwards believed had been the person to cause all the mischief to be done to his property.

This person was very likely one of the farmers involved, since magistrates were Protestants of that class. Beatson therefore had a grievance against them, and it was he who showed Gray a copy of the bill. But why did he have a copy of the bill? It is a surprise to find Beatson speaking out against the Barra 'establishment', since in 1851 he had been actively involved in rounding people up for expulsion on an emigrant ship, for the proprietor, John Gordon of Cluny.

Father MacDonnell, the priest, 'believes that the most valuable part of the property saved from the "Annie Jane" was never brought to sale at all.'

Gray's report confirms what has long been suspected in Barra, that the MacLellans and MacGillivray were involved in selling the booty. The MacLellans are mentioned by name in the song (Appendix 5), and the words 'loaded their carts and travelled to the north' are thought to refer to MacGillivray's farm at Eoligarry. The question of exactly who was collecting the jewellery – a grisly task which involved cutting or biting fingers off dead bodies to get the rings off – remains uncertain (see Appendix 5). It is a sensitive issue in Barra and Vatersay to this day; the tradition is that the inhabitants of Vatersay at the time were incomers and mostly Protestants, but there is an unwillingness to offend Barra Protestants by blaming those incomers.

The report on the loss of the *Annie Jane* concluded that it was not just the unusually severe equinoctial gales that finished her; it was her heavy cargo and the way in which it had been stowed which caused her to roll so violently that some of the masts literally snapped off. The crew was insufficient in number and competence, and included eighteen Canadians who were afraid to climb the rigging to furl sails during storms, which led to the loss of sails and masts. There is no reference in the report to subsequent suggestions that the captain mistook Bàgh Siar for the

Sound of Vatersay. It is unlikely that he would have attempted to navigate such a narrow channel in a storm, in the dark, with a practically uncontrollable ship.

'Extraordinary stories regarding this wreck' circulated in subsequent years, according to a visitor in 1887: 'The marks and wounds on the bodies of those cast up on the beach gave rise to the report that some of the passengers and crew met with violence or foul play at the hands of the islanders, and no people have felt the accusation more keenly than the inhabitants of Vatersay and Barra. That there was plunder no one denies, and the sailors of the ship were implicated also. The story that the crofters of Vatersay were all removed by Government on account of their conduct towards the emigrants is at once disposed of by the fact that the islanders were evicted long previous to make way for sheep . . . traces of their houses can still be seen.'[5]

Although the above-mentioned Thomas Gray recorded a lot of detail about the *Annie Jane,* he had been sent to Barra in August 1866 following concerns raised by the Committee of Lloyds about the conduct of officials with regard to recent wrecks. The *Bermuda*, en route from Dumbarton to Trinidad, was wrecked on the last day of 1865 on the south coast of Vatersay, east of Bàgh a' Deas. She was carrying coal, bricks, seed oats and huge pans to contain sugar cane on the homeward voyage. Her captain, Alexander Coulter, complained about the conduct of the Deputy Receiver of Wreck, Neil MacDonald from South Uist, who charged him a large fee for services rendered, when he had rendered practically no services and had not made Coulter aware that he had any services to offer, let alone responsibilities to fulfil. Gray was informed that 'with the snow thick on the ground, the captain's wife had her garments taken off her back and his children had their shoes taken off their feet and nothing was done to punish the offenders or to stop the plundering.'

As in the case of the *Annie Jane*, exactly who was doing this plundering is not clear; practically all the thirty-two inhabitants recorded in the 1861 population census were incomers, from South Uist, Harris, Skye, Coll and the mainland. By 1866 Archibald MacLellan, born in South Uist, had taken over the farm from Donald MacLellan, who was still in charge in 1861. Gray had this to say about MacDonald:

The representative of the Board of Trade appears to be a very bad character. He allows wrecked property to be plundered in the most reckless manner, and himself in some instances shares the plunder. The office of Receiver in his hands has been used as a means, not of protecting the interests of owners, but of extorting money for himself.

This Deputy gets intoxicated and a very laughable circumstance was told of him by the Catholic Priest. He says that on one occasion the Deputy went to bed 'intoxicated' but not drunk. He had some money with him and placed it for security in the chamber utensil [pot]. Someone else sleeping in the same room was about to touch it when a very unseemly but curious squabble arose as to the right of possession.

Gray reported that 'derelict vessels abandoned during their voyage to or from our North American Provinces are continually washed ashore' on the Barra Isles. A week after the wreck of the *Bermuda*, one such, the *Harmony,* drifting bottom up, met her end on one of the skerries off the south-east coast of Vatersay. She was carrying timber, stamped with the name of a company in Quebec; timber was a valuable commodity on treeless islands, but of greater financial value were the copper bolts holding her together. Gray wrote, 'The labour in getting the copper bolts out of this vessel must have been considerable. They all had to be hammered out from the outside with driving pins and sledge hammers. It must have been a work not of hours or days, but of weeks. Some of the driving pins are left about the wreck by the people who stole the bolts . . . it became quite evident to me that no plunder could have taken place if the slightest attempt had been made to stop it.'

Between the arrival of the *Bermuda* and *Harmony,* another 'derelict' hit Sandray. She broke up and her cargo of paraffin in barrels came ashore on Vatersay – probably on the beach of Bàgh a' Deas – near where the *Bermuda* was wrecked two days before. The barrels were from Philadelphia, USA. Seventy barrels, of which the Deputy Receiver reported only fifty, were stored next to a wall near Vatersay House. A witness reported that 'I saw the people [of Barra] burning the paraffin, in all kinds of vessels extemporised for the occasion, one having it in a teapot, the wick through the spout. I saw some more [barrels] on the island of Sandera; all of these I heard were later stolen.'

Gray made some serious allegations about the conduct of the Roman Catholic priest, William MacDonnell:

They fear him because 'he can turn them into a pillar of salt' and they hate him most cordially because he levies such a large percentage on their earnings. On the occasion of the wreck of the 'Alfaretta' on Barra the priest attended when Captain Grant paid the men, and took his share from them. He charges, so I am informed, £5 for some rite in connection with the burial of the dead, and the relations of the dead are in his debt for a year or two afterwards. The priests in South Uist are very much scandalized by his proceedings but they are powerless to remove him . . . The Procurator Fiscal was sent once to admonish the priest for a part he had taken in some wreck matter, and the priest took him in and made him drunk and then turned him out to be howled at and pulled about by the people his followers.

I little thought that so much poverty or rascality could exist anywhere, as exists in Barra. The wretched people live in huts with their animals and are half washed and covered in vermin. So much for the poverty, but the lying and rascality are something too bad to describe, and our Deputy Receiver is, with the exception perhaps of the Catholic Priest, the biggest wrecker and liar of the lot. The policeman is a drunken useless man, he takes part with the people instead of preventing plunder.

Gray was struck by the clothing worn by the women in Barra:

For clothing the women seem to wear all sorts of odd things. They do not appear to me to wear as a rule clothes of home manufacture and of native wool but to have a selection from a most marvellous miscellaneous collection of old clothes, specimens of costume that would correspond with almost any costume from Queen Anne's time downwards. The only conclusion I can come to is that they get their clothes from wrecks. The one drawback is that through being slept in on the ground at night, and getting wet all day, the garment loses its distinctive colour and pattern, and all alike seem to be dirty, draggled and deplorable . . . The men dressed better than the women, they wore sailors' or fishermens' ordinary clothes of varied colour and make. But some of the elders seemed to indulge only in dirt and pigtail. They stood at the doorways of their huts secure from the cold in a covering of dirt with their heads in the smoke from the peat fire (the door serves as the chimney).

Gray's report on Barra and Vatersay was based on a visit of only two days, and some of its content is not borne out by other evidence. In Barra tradition William MacDonnell is remembered with respect, and he supervised the rebuilding of the Parish Church of St Brendan at Craigston. As a result of the report, and evidence from others involved, MacDonald and his superior, based at Stornoway, and the policeman (Alexander MacLeod, not a native of Barra), were sacked. They were aggrieved that they had had no chance to defend themselves against allegations which were not revealed to them. Gray published a very watered down version of his report, disguising it as an account of Barra, in a monthly magazine, *Nature and Art*. He omitted nearly all the critical – libellous, in effect – references to individuals except for some unflattering remarks about MacLeod. The article found its way to Barra where MacLeod was, understandably, outraged, and threatened legal action against Gray.[6]

There were several other wrecks on Vatersay in the later nineteenth century. In February 1854 the *W.H. Davis,* en route from Liverpool to New Orleans, was wrecked with the loss of thirty crew. She had sailed from Liverpool on 10 January, but put into Belfast only two days later, on account of the crew refusing to work because she was leaking. New pumps were fitted and she continued her journey. *The Scotsman* (11 February 1854) reported on her demise: 'The moment the ill-fated ship touched the rock, the master and crew took to the rigging, expecting, no doubt, that as the ship heeled over, they would be able to gain the rocks. In a few minutes the ship was dashed to pieces, and the whole of the poor fellows fell amid the wreck and perished. Only one escaped, the steward. He took refuge on the bowsprit, and as the vessel went to pieces he sprang forward, and succeeded in reaching the rocks in safety, although very much bruised. Several bodies of the crew were discovered among the rocks by the fishermen, who conveyed them to Vatersay for interment.'

This could be the same event recounted by Kate Gillies of Caolas more than a century later. She said that the sole survivor had been ill and climbed along the bowsprit to safety. He crawled to a shepherd's house at Caolas, so the ship must have struck somewhere on the north coast. Kate Gillies also told the story of another ship, the *Rose Anne* of Belfast wrecked at Caolas, in which two dead men were found and 'half the body of a man was hanging from the mast.'[7]

In December 1875 The *Mount Royal*, carrying coal, was

wrecked in Bàgh Bhatarsaigh. According to *The Scotsman* (12 February 1876), 'The vessel sailed from the Clyde on 12 November, but when half way across the Atlantic had to put back, the seamen refusing to perform duty, and afterwards went ashore in Vatersay Bay,' having struck the sunken rock, Sgeir Vichalea, and then being run ashore in an inlet somewhere between Gortein and Beannachan.

The brigantine *Fanny* sailing from Greenock with a cargo of coal, brown sugar and beer, sought shelter in Bàgh Bhatarsaigh during a gale, but dragged anchor and was driven ashore on the north side of the bay. She was salvaged and advertised for sale in Stornoway in *The Scotsman* of 6 July 1882.

No doubt many vessels had come to grief on Vatersay's shores in earlier times. A writer in 1908 suggested that not all wrecks were accidents: 'these sands [of Traigh Siar, West Beach] have been dreadfully profitable in the past. In the earlier decades of the last century wreckers found Vatersay a charmed spot. Treacherous lights blazing lured vessels onto the sandy reef.' These 'lights' could have been quite innocent – they may have been the fires of kelp ovens. An undesirable consequence of shipwrecks was rats, and it was reported in 1888 that 'Vatersay is teeming with them.'[8] This observation was made by John Finlayson, school teacher on Mingulay, which had managed to remain rat-free; Vatersay was no worse than Barra or Sandray in terms of rat-infestation.

Returning to the farm, by 1866 Archibald MacLellan had taken over as farmer, as noted above. The earliest detailed map of Vatersay dates from this period, 1861–63. In addition to Vatersay House, which had an extension at the north side of the back, and the steading, there were three other single buildings. These were: above the shore at Cuithir, at the south-west corner of Bàgh Bhatarsaigh; at Gortein, where ruins can be seen above the road east of the 1927 school building; and at Caolas, at the narrowest point of the sound. There was a road between the machair at Gortein and the landing place at Uidh, and another between the steading and the building at Cuithir.[9]

Vatersay was transformed in the 1860s when a herring curing station was established on the south side of Bàgh Bhatarsaigh. Local tradition is that it got going before Castlebay was developed as a herring station in about 1867, by curers from the east coast of Scotland who had the large boats and netting required. Vatersay was classed as a station along with Castlebay, Lochboisdale and Lochmaddy. In the 1868 season, when records begin, 107 boats, crewed by 642 men and boys were based there. There were thirty-three coopers, and 267 gutters and packers – women who gutted the herrings and packed them in barrels with salt. The station produced 800 tons of herrings which were carried to market – Russia and ports on the Baltic and North Sea coasts – by fifty men. In all, about 1,000 people on an island with only a couple of dozen permanent inhabitants! The workers, from the islands and some from the east coast, were employed by curers from the east coasts of Scotland and England. They based themselves there during the season, May and June, and thereafter operations were transferred northwards along the Outer Hebrides, following the migrating herring, and then down the east coasts of Scotland and England. Thomas Brown and Son, fish curers in Lowestoft, Suffolk, advertised in *The Scotsman* in March 1875: 'Thirty boats and crews wanted to engage to fish at

Vatersay from 18 May to 24 June.' In 1883 there were twelve curers at Vatersay, and thirty-three at Castlebay. The 1878 Ordnance Survey map shows small buildings – wooden huts – strung out along the south shore of the bay for about a kilometre (half a mile), as far as the saddle leading to Eorasdail, and platforms marking the sites of huts can be seen above the shore. The two photographs of the herring station (plates 3 and 4) were taken at about this time. In the cemetery in Vatersay there is a memorial to two brothers, Joseph and John Thomson, Roman Catholics from Branderburgh, Moray, who were drowned while working from the station in 1875.

A visitor in 1887 arrived on a vessel supplying the station with fish curing stock. He noted that open air services were held for Protestant fishermen on Sundays during the season, and that Mr MacDonald, the farmer from 1883, 'is a favourite with those engaged in the herring trade, and from his house supplies of milk are got at a reasonable rate.'

The Vatersay station operated until 1892, and the tradition is that it was abandoned because of sand drift during a storm. Perhaps the fact that the 1892 herring season in Barra was, according to *The Scotsman* of 12 July 1892, 'a total failure and some curers have lost heavily' had something to do with it. During the heyday of the industry in Barra, not long afterwards, it was said that Castle Bay was so crowded with boats that it would have been possible to walk to Vatersay over them.[10]

At the time of the population census taken in April 1871, five fishermen from Aberdeenshire were occupying a fisherman's hut; this was too early in the year for herring but they could have been catching cod or ling. There were only seventeen permanent residents of Vatersay at the time: MacLellan and ten employees in Vatersay House, and the family of Alexander MacDonald, a herd from South Uist. They may have been living at Caolas, since it is known that they were doing so thirty years later. A decade later there was little change, although there were two new farm employees, living in two separate houses. The total population was nineteen. Sometime between the maps of 1861–63 and 1878 an extension on the south side of the back of Vatersay House was built.

A visitor described Vatersay in 1882 as 'rented by Mr M'Lellan, one of the most extensive stock rearers in the Long Island; and some of the pasturage over which we passed while we were on shore looked to be of the sweetest and most succulent description'.[11]

MacLellan's lease expired in 1883, and forty-five cottars from Castlebay appealed to the landowner, Lady Gordon Cathcart, for crofts on Vatersay. John Gordon, son of Colonel John who had bought the islands in 1840, died in 1878, leaving the estate to his widow. He had married Emily Eliza Steele Pringle in 1865 when he was 45, she 20. She was born in India where her father was in the Madras civil service, and raised in Roxburghshire. Her mother was a niece of Alexander MacNeil of Colonsay; the MacNeils had been lairds since 1701, when one of the MacNeils of Knapdale (Kintyre) bought Colonsay, and there may have been a remote connection with the MacNeils of Barra. After her husband's death she married Sir Reginald Cathcart of Killochan Castle, Ayr, and styled herself Lady Gordon Cathcart. She visited her dominions in the year of her accession, but never again in her fifty-four-year rule. She declined the cottars' request for Vater-

say, and the farm was leased to another farmer, Donald Mac-
Donald. He had come from the family farm at Allasdale, Barra,
which he was obliged to leave in 1883 as Lady Cathcart divided it
up into crofts. The family was originally from North Uist,
Donald's father Archibald being one of those who arrived during
the 1830s to take up farms created by evicting crofters. Donald's
brother, Archibald, was the Church of Scotland minister of Barra
for sixty-one years from 1871. A sister, Ann, and her husband
John Ferguson, a shepherd, settled at the west end of Caolas,
Vatersay, on the machair between Traigh Bharlais and Port a'
Bhàta. By 1891 MacDonald had married, and he and his wife had
four children as well as their own mothers living with them in
Vatersay House, along with twelve employees. MacDonald
regularly sent cattle and sheep to be sold at the Stirling sales.[12]

Two of the MacDonald children, plus four other local children, were described as scholars in the population census of 1891,
but no resident teacher was recorded. In 1894 Barra School Board
discussed the need for a school for the island, and a so-called 'side
school' or 'sub school' of Castlebay School opened in 1895. The
Castlebay School log-book recorded in March 1896 that the head
teacher, James Smith, visited the Vatersay school and 'seven pupils
were present and on being examined in the various subjects
professed they gave every evidence of being diligently taught.'
The annual inspection took place in May and the children
'acquitted themselves creditably', as they did in subsequent
inspections, but no more detail is given. The school was probably
held in a room in the southern extension at the back of Vatersay
House, labelled 'old schoolroom' on a plan of 1910. The last
recorded annual inspection was in July 1900 but the teacher,

Malcolm MacDonald, was still there at the time of the census of 1901, living in Vatersay House, and six children were described as scholars. The school must have closed shortly afterwards.[13]

The golden jubilee of Victoria's reign was celebrated in grand style on Vatersay. *The Scotsman* of 27 June 1887 reported: 'Under the patronage of Commander J.W. Osborne, Lieutenant Maltby and officers of HMS *Jackal*, jubilee sports were held on the Island of Vatersay on Saturday, it was a delightful day and over 1,000 people were present. The races were principally performed by the crew of the *Jackal* and some of them were open to all comers. Three cheers were given to Her Majesty the Queen.'

This would seem to be an incongruous event for Vatersay, with only a handful of inhabitants, and 1,000 people would represent nearly half the population of Barra; but as it was held during the herring fishing season, when several thousand workers descended on Barra and Vatersay, these workers must have made up the majority of the spectators.

The fifty years from 1850 were a curious interlude in Vatersay's history. The crofters were thrown out, and farmers and workers from other islands were brought in. There were many shipwrecks, including that of the *Annie Jane*, one of the worst maritime disasters on the coast of Scotland. For about twenty-five years, a herring curing station employing up to 1,000 people flourished for a couple of months each year. Cottars from Barra attempted to get crofts on Vatersay for the first time in 1883, and this theme was to dominate the first decade of the next century.

4. Early raids, 1900–1906

By 1900, when the main raiding period began, Vatersay had only been inhabited by successive tenants of Vatersay Farm and their workers for fifty years. The green pastures were enjoyed exclusively by sheep and cattle which were more profitable than the crofters who had lived there before being evicted from the island. When sheep farms were created in Barra, the evicted crofters had been resettled onto inferior land on the east coast. Throughout the nineteenth century the population of Barra had been growing, but the amount of land available to the majority had shrunk, because people had been forced off the better land to make way for sheep. Before 1883 very few new crofts had been created (although some had been sub-divided by tenants), so the result was a growing number of families with no land at all. These people, in most cases the children of crofters, were known as 'cottars'. They eked out a living by fishing, and borrowing bits of relatives' crofts for growing potatoes and grazing a cow. They built houses – 'cot-houses', hence the term cottar – on relatives' crofts, or on common grazing land. In the Castlebay area where conditions were worst – 'congested' was the term used – many cottars lived in wooden huts by the shore. The factor (estate manager) did not, in his words, want 'ugly wooden erections alongside the road', yet even when people applied for sites for stone houses with slate roofs, they were turned down. Water was often taken from surface sources which could be contaminated, and infectious diseases were common.[1]

To the south, across Castle Bay, lay the green and pleasant and empty land of Vatersay. In February 1883 the lease of the farm of Vatersay was due for renewal, and 45 cottars and crofters from Glen and Castlebay wrote to the landowner, Lady Gordon Cathcart, requesting that she make the island available for crofting. Three of the cottars actually travelled to her main residence, Cluny Castle in Aberdeenshire, in an attempt to put their case to her in person, but they had to make do with a meeting with her secretary, Ranald MacDonald. In her reply (from another of her residences, Titness Park in Berkshire) to John MacLean and forty-four other applicants, Lady Cathcart stated, 'I regret that I do not see my way to accept your offer; but, although it is not usual for a proprietor to give reasons why an offer for a farm has been declined, I think it right to make you aware of some of the reasons which have influenced me.'

She then gave her reasons. Firstly, she maintained that the island's water supply was inadequate in dry weather. Secondly, she had recently invested large sums of money in developing Castlebay as a fishing port by building a pier and a hotel for fish curers from the mainland to stay in during the herring season. Many of the cottars were fishermen and would have benefited from these developments, as well as from the school recently built in Castlebay by Barra School Board. If Vatersay were to be settled by crofting families they would need a water supply, a school, church and infrastructure such as paths and jetties. Thirdly, she doubted that the cottars would be able to afford to build houses or to stock their crofts with cattle and sheep. Fourthly, she doubted their ability to pay the rent for their crofts, citing the example of an island crofting community, Mingulay, where many crofters had not paid rent for over ten years. She also maintained that Vatersay had never been occupied by crofters, because she claimed (wrongly) that there was no evidence of it in the estate documents from the MacNeil era. However, there should have been records from 1840 when her first husband's father took over, because he had evicted the last of them only thirty-three years earlier. 'I have come to the conclusion,' she pronounced, 'that it would be a great mistake to plant a crofter population in the isolated island of Vatersay.'

Lady Cathcart was not, however, completely negative in her response. She wanted to encourage the fishing industry, but she felt that fishermen should work full time – on their own account and for the fish curers during the herring season in May and June – and not be distracted by croft work. She wanted the fishermen to adopt the model of her fishing tenants on the coast of Aberdeenshire, who were fishing full time. To this end she proposed creating small allotments for the fishermen for growing potatoes and keeping a cow; sheep were to be kept on the remainder of the land, which was to be used as common grazing. She created these allotments in two areas in the vicinity of Castlebay which had hitherto been let as grazing for the large farms: Bentangaval, formerly used by Vatersay Farm, where forty-five allotments were to be created; and Garrygall, formerly used by Eoligarry Farm, which would have forty. The fishermen were to live in the designated fishing hamlets of Castlebay, Kentangaval, and Glen, the reasoning being that boat crews should live close together so as to be able to set out early in the morning together.

The two experimental schemes were begun later in 1883. Giving evidence to the so-called 'Deer Forest Commission' in 1894, Ranald MacDonald, Lady Cathcart's secretary, stated that 'the results of these experiments have been extremely disappointing.' At Bentangaval, only thirty-five cottars applied, so that the rent for each allotment had to be higher than envisaged. Many of the tenants failed to keep up their rent payments; only one-seventh of the total due in the first eight years was paid. The stock was not managed properly and the grazing was not used to advantage. At Garrygall, where the tenants came from Glen and a few from Mingulay, some tenants built houses on their allotments, which was expressly forbidden. The failure, as the estate saw it, of these schemes reinforced its negative attitude to the cottars; however, as one of the commissioners pointed out to Mr MacDonald, 'might it not be possible that had you experimented according to the desires of the people themselves your experiment might have been more successful?' The estate seemed to be unable to understand that full-time fishing was never a possibility in Barra because of the stormy sea conditions, the lack of suitable boats, and the distance from markets. The custom in Barra was to combine crofting, fishing and paid employment when available, that being the only way to survive. Furthermore, forcing the tenants to live some distance from their allotments was not conducive to good management.

In 1892, forty-seven cottars wrote to Lady Cathcart stating that before the passing of the Crofters Act of 1886, '. . . many of our neighbours had been in the habit of giving us the privilege of the use of a small patch of potato land and a little grazing for our small stock by which with what little work we could get and the gathering of shellfish we were enabled to eke out a livelihood; but . . . we are informed that the crofters cannot be allowed to give us any potato land or grazing without incurring the forfeiture of their tenancy, and we are thus placed in the position of starvation facing us in the future . . . We humbly petition your ladyship to give our petition your favourable consideration.'[2]

The estate response to Donald MacIntyre (one of the raiders in 1906) and forty-six others was, predictably, negative. The cottars had also been allowed to grow potatoes on Vatersay, as a report in *The Scotsman* of 22 May 1886 shows: 'A number of the Barra crofters [cottars was meant] who last year were granted, though reluctantly, potato ground on the island of Vatersay by the tenant, have this year forcibly taken possession of the same land, in spite of protests from the tenant who is thus deprived of the best part of his farm.' The tenant farmer was Donald MacDonald who granted land for this purpose some years later. This raid – in other words, illegal seizing of land – is the first recorded in the Barra Isles and one of the earliest anywhere in the region. It was no doubt inspired by recent raids in Sutherland, Benbecula and Tiree, and more followed, in Skye and Lewis. The immediate cause of these raids was the failure of the Crofters' Act of 1886 to address the needs of cottars by making provision for the creation of more crofts; it had benefited crofters by giving them security of tenure and compensating them for improvements they had made. However, there

were deeper underlying factors: in some cases, these were griev-
ances over land from which landlords had evicted crofters years
before, and turned into sheep farms. With a rising population, the
descendants of those evicted needed land, and they wanted 'their'
land back. In other cases landlords had taken back land which was
previously common grazing for crofters' sheep. In this first Vatersay case, the raid was about being denied potato ground which
they had been granted the previous year, although by this time
they had already appealed for crofts on the island. Raiding became
a means of landless people demanding land over a period of about
forty years in the Hebrides.

The cottars' case for crofts in Vatersay was strengthened by the
Deer Forest Commission, which in 1894 designated the island as
suitable for crofting. The same year, Barra Parish Council
appealed to Inverness-shire County Council for allotments using
the provisions of the Allotments (Scotland) Act of 1892. The Act
was aimed at the so-called 'labouring classes' of which there were
very few representatives in Barra, but its potential was not lost on
the islanders. Cottars from Castlebay, Glen and Brevig applied,
through the Parish Council, for allotments in various places,
including Vatersay. The Allotments Committee of the County
Council visited Barra and recommended that plots of four acres
should be leased for a trial period of ten years, but the County
Council as a whole did not support the recommendation, and
the scheme was shelved in 1899. Meanwhile the Congested
Districts Board had been established in 1897, with a remit to buy
land for crofting – although it did not have powers of compulsory purchase – and promote agriculture, fishing and other
economic development.[3]

It is easy to appreciate the frustration of cottars around Castlebay who had for years attempted to obtain crofts or, failing that, allotments or, third best, the loan of land for growing potatoes. The failure of the allotments appeal must have spurred the cottars to approach the Vatersay farmer, Donald MacDonald, again for the loan of potato ground. In the spring of 1900 he granted them the use of land at Caolas. While this was welcome, it was not a permanent solution. The frustration of cottars in northern Barra reached boiling point on 8 September 1900, when they raided part of the farm of Northbay. This was probably a tactic not only to put pressure on the estate, but also to get the Congested Districts Board involved.[4]

Following the example of these raiders, about forty cottars, all men, from Kentangaval, Garrygall and Glen, raided Caolas on Vatersay, on 22 September 1900. This was the first of the raids which took place almost every year until 1906, when the raiders began to build huts and take up residence on the island. In a statement to the police at Castlebay, the farm manager Archibald MacRae (nephew of Donald MacDonald), named nineteen culprits who were 'measuring off allotments or crofts and house sites for themselves and putting stones on end between the lots, to mark off the marches . . . if they persevere in this illegal course and disturbing the stock, I wish them prosecuted.' The constable noted that 'they intended to warn Donald MacDonald to remove his stock by Martinmas [11 November]. They are determined to proceed no matter the consequences.' The cottars, whose leader was Roderick Gillies of Garrygall, marked out twenty-one crofts.[5]

Two days later, twenty cottars delivered a letter to Ranald MacDonald, Lady Cathcart's secretary. They appealed to him to give them crofts on Vatersay and threatened to take possession if a favourable answer was not received within fifteen days. Five hundred people were reported to have assembled in Castlebay to await a response; when it came, it was not favourable. Cottars again raided Caolas on 1 October and marked out a further fifteen crofts. Writing in the *Daily Free Press* of the 1 October, MacDonald disputed the hardships claimed to have been suffered by the cottars, and reiterated the usual points about the estate's investments in the fishing industry in Castlebay, the failed Bentangaval and Garrygall schemes, and its views on crofting. He also accused the area's Liberal Party candidate in the forthcoming general election, John Dewar, of supporting the raiders and their cause in order to gain votes. He claimed that 'the Barra cottars are in a state of feverish excitement, which in a most extraordinary way has been fanned into a flame by glaring misrepresentations contained in a report in "The Highland News" sent by Wilson of Lochmaddy' (Thomas Wilson, Dewar's agent). He also called for police action to restore order in the islands, as had happened in other areas.[6]

The cottars raided Vatersay again in February 1901, having spent the interval at the herring fishing on the east coast of Scotland. This time the target of nine raiders was the peninsula of Uidh, where they marked off 'crofts' along the shore facing Castlebay and gathered seaweed in preparation for spreading it on the ground as fertiliser for potatoes. Among them was Duncan Campbell of Kentangaval, who was to become the leader of the raiders; he had not been one of the raiders the previous September. The Procurator-Fiscal told the raiders of Vatersay and of Northbay Farm to desist as it would be 'ungrateful' to Scottish Secretary Lord Balfour of Burleigh who was trying to obtain land for them from Lady Cathcart.[7]

In March 1901 there was jubilation among the cottars of northern Barra when the Congested Districts Board announced the purchase of Northbay Farm and part of Eoligarry Farm from Lady Gordon Cathcart, for the creation of fifty-eight crofts in four townships: Northbay, Cliat, Grean, and Eoligarry. There was no cause for rejoicing among the raiders of Vatersay, however, although the success of the raiding of Northbay must have encouraged them; it also encouraged land raiding in the Uists and Lewis. Donald MacDonald allowed them the use of potato ground at Caolas again, but if this was an attempt to forestall further raiding, it didn't work. On 1 April, twenty-four cottars walked over the land between Uidh and the farm buildings and marked off crofts 'on land which had been out of cultivation for many years, placing stones between rigs to mark the marches between lots.'[8]

The population census of Vatersay at this time (March 1901) recorded twenty-seven inhabitants in four households. Donald MacDonald lived in Vatersay House with family members and employees, as well as Malcolm MacDonald, the teacher. Six island children were described as 'scholars', and he taught in an annexe of Vatersay House. Farm grieve Archibald McCuish and his family lived nearby. Ann Ferguson, widowed sister of Donald MacDonald, lived with her family at the west end of Caolas. A family of MacDonalds including Alexander and Archibald, shepherds, lived on the neck of the peninsula of Beinn Orosaidh at Caolas. These three families all stayed on and became crofters after 1909.

In March of the following year, 1902, cottars (among whom were two women) again raided Vatersay when their appeals to Donald MacDonald for potato ground were refused. They had written to Lord Balfour to advise him of their intentions ten days before. They said they would not relinquish the land until instructed to by him. His response was to instruct the police to issue warnings to the raiders, which some of them must have ignored because the police charged them with taking illegal possession of land. In the meantime many of them had attended a meeting in Castlebay of the Land League, a movement which fought for the rights of crofters and cottars. Duncan Campbell proposed seizing land if potato ground was refused, but more moderate voices counselled against, an indication of the diversity of views among the cottars.[9]

By the autumn of 1902 the cottars were desperate; the fishing had been poor that year, they had been unable to grow potatoes in Vatersay, and crofters in Barra who had previously granted potato ground to cottars had also withdrawn the offer. Earlier in the year the Congested Districts Board had attempted to rent land from Donald MacDonald for the cottars to use for growing potatoes, but this had failed, so the Board requested Lady Cathcart to sell it some land. This she was quite happy to do as it fitted in with her belief that fishermen should have potato plots but not crofts as such. In January 1903 the Board bought sixty acres of the Uidh peninsula for the exorbitant sum of £600. The area bought was the end of the peninsula known as Uidh Gheal, east of the line of the current fence at Caraigrigh. It included the beaches (where seaweed could be gathered for fertiliser), the hilly area, called Creag Mhòr, and the tidal island of

Uinessan. The Board had received a favourable report on the suitability of the land for potato growing. About fifty cottar families rented plots, and Duncan Campbell was responsible for collecting the rents.[10]

The purchase of the potato ground provided temporary relief for the cottars, and there were no raids in the spring of 1903; early spring was the usual raiding season, being a slack time in the crofting and fishing calendar. However, the cottars complained about the quality of the soil, following a poor potato harvest, and raiding was resumed in 1904 and 1905. The Chief Constable of Inverness-shire, A. MacHardy, wearily noted: 'The usual fuss among the cottars over the annual spring planting of potatoes has aroused the excitement.' In February 1905 the cottars threatened to seize Vatersay before the negotiations for the renewal of the farmer's lease the following year began. Duncan Campbell, who was by now referred to as 'the leader in this agitation', wrote direct to Lady Cathcart on behalf of sixty-two cottars, appealing for crofts to be created after the expiry of the farmer's lease, but he got no reply. It is not known if Campbell had been involved previously in 'agitation', but he gave evidence to the Deer Forest Commission in 1894.[11]

In March 1905 the Congested Districts Board asked one of its own experts to assess the potato land. He reported:

The soil is all over of poor quality. I do not consider that any part of it is suitable for growing potatoes . . . the people state that about 47 years ago potatoes were planted two years in succession in this place with exactly the same results; that had they known that the Board intended to buy this part for them they would have warned them against it . . . they had determined to give it a fair trial and had thoroughly manured the land with seaweed. They promised not to seize any part of the island this year, as they believed the Board would help them if it could, but would make no such promise with regard to next year . . . I found the people very reasonable in their talk and their demands . . . the want of potatoes among 47 families must be a very great hardship especially when those who went to Glasgow to get work for the winter were unable to find such.[12]

It is curious that there was a memory of poor results from Creag Mhòr in 1858, since at that time most of the inhabitants were incomers who did not stay long, and it is not known that anyone was living in that area then. The lack of work in Glasgow was due to a serious industrial depression in 1904–1905, and as the report shows, the effects were felt in the remotest areas.

The Board took soil samples which were analysed by a chemist, who confirmed that the soil was poor. It also proposed conducting experiments in growing potatoes on the land, but the cottars would not cooperate, probably because they had already requested the Board to acquire more suitable land and they did not want that process to be delayed. In expectation of having better land, many of them had not planted potatoes on Creag Mhòr in the spring of 1905.[13]

In November 1905 Duncan Campbell wrote to the Board referring to the letter he had written to them in April about getting crofts on Vatersay, but which had not been answered (the

Board claimed it could not trace it). 'We are getting weary . . . in the month of January we are just going to have our dwellings put up there and be within reach of the land unless we get word at once'.[14]

A month later Campbell wrote to Donald MacDonald, the farmer, having heard that he, MacDonald, was going to let his cattle onto the potato ground of Creag Mhòr:

> We are advising you not to open the gate to let in any of them, for when the place was bought for us we were not in a mind to let Vatersay have it again but that we would have the rest of Vatersay with it and we are in that mind yet . . . we would want a bit of land for potato planting in the spring, after that date we are in mind to take possession of the whole place, and we advise you to be looking for some other place that will be suitable for you. We were not hating and are not hating you yet, but as is natural we put ourselves first so you need not doubt any of this for this is our mind and nothing but it.[15]

The crudeness and tone of this letter contrasts with the eloquence of the raiders' letters in later years, which were written by Neil MàcPhee of Mingulay. Campbell also wrote to the Board suggesting that they 'should acquire for us the land of Vatersay and have it cut up into suitable lots for the worst cases of congestion around Castlebay.' The Board replied that 'even if the proprietor would sell the island, which is very doubtful, the Board has no funds for further land purchases.'[16]

The following month, January 1906, the Board's representative in Barra, Donald Monk, met with Donald MacDonald, the farmer, John MacDonald, the estate factor (and the farmer's nephew), and Duncan Campbell, in order to negotiate for some more suitable potato ground. John MacDonald, in a letter to the Board's secretary, R. MacGregor, stated that Donald MacDonald kindly allowed Campbell to choose the land, and his choice was more land on the Uidh peninsula, adjacent to Creag Mhòr. He stated that when MacDonald made the offer, 'Duncan Campbell, who was most unreasonable and uncourteous in every way, began to make various conditions which on no consideration could be agreed to.'

John MacDonald and Monk walked over Creag Mhòr to consider the proposed experiment in potato growing, and to their surprise they found some of the previous year's crop which had not been lifted. MacDonald wrote to MacGregor:

To our amazement we found that the potatoes were of an excellent crop, although in discussing the matter with Duncan Campbell earlier in the day he stoutly denied that potatoes would grow there. We took samples of the potatoes, and Mr Monk intends forwarding a sample to the Board which I hope will be sufficient proof that the ground is quite suitable, and it may show that a further experiment is not absolutely necessary, especially when it is taken into account that the cottars will be certain to show hostility and would probably endeavour to do something to make the experiment a failure. Considering the manner in which these cottars carry out the cultivation of the soil it would be no wonder if potatoes would not grow. They commence work in the month of April by spreading any sort of rubbishy seaweed, sometimes as dry as shavings, on the ground and plant the potatoes immediately thereafter, the seed used being generally the refuse of the former season's crop. It is perfectly well known by every person in Castlebay that no further attention is shown either in the way of weeding or drilling the potatoes, and the consequence is that by the time they are ripe they are practically on the surface. Taking all these things into consideration it says a good deal for the quality of the soil that any return at all should be got, and it appears to me very strange that the cottars should be hushing the matter up and making statements to the Board as to the unsuitability of the soil.[17]

On the basis of this letter, MacGregor wrote to Campbell on 5 February 1906, quoting some of these criticisms, saying that the Board would not proceed with the proposed acquisition of additional potato ground. A few weeks later, however, the Board had to do a U-turn.

On the same day that MacGregor wrote to Campbell, the cottars stepped up their campaign for their ultimate goal: the whole island of Vatersay. Carrying spades and preceded by a piper, forty-three cottars landed at Uidh and walked along the track towards the farm. They assembled in a field of stubble on the south side of the farm steading – a rough square of barns and byres where the southernmost houses of the township of Vatersay now are – and proceeded to mark off fourteen 'crofts'. They shouted their jubilation at having got the land at last. They spent about an hour there and then returned to Castlebay.[18]

Two days later, presumably when Duncan Campbell received MacGregor's letter, thirty angry cottars raided the land they had just been informed they were not going to get, and marked off potato plots. The police advised the cottars to desist. A week after that, cottars returned to the south of the island and marked off a further forty crofts south-east of the steading. There were, therefore, two issues being pursued in these raids: the demand for crofts, and the demand for potato ground.[19]

The raids were widely reported in the Scottish press, more so than any other raids of the period, reinforcing the raiders' own view that these were the beginning of a more determined struggle. The raiders, or their supporters, may have engineered the publicity partly to send a signal to the new Liberal government. *The Daily Record and Mail* of 10 February suggested that 'Vatersay may yet become a place famous in history.' *The Scotsman* of 8 February speculated whether the raids could be 'the portent and prelude to another Hebridean crofters' storm.' Both predictions turned out to be prophetic. *The Scotsman* took the chance to have a dig at the new government: 'A government which has not the means or the courage to grasp the Land Problem by the horns may see an opportunity of taking it by the tail – at Vatersay, the very fag-end of the King's dominions.'

Within a few weeks the Congested Districts Board negotiated with Donald MacDonald to rent the potato land under dispute: twenty acres at Caraigrigh, adjacent to the land already bought. Part of the agreement was that the tenant relied on the government preventing further invasion of the farm. On learning this,

Scottish Office officials were surprised, since they regarded the matter as a case for the proprietor to deal with, indicating that the Board and the Scottish Office were not always on the same wavelength. They were not persuaded by Lady Cathcart's solicitors to 'put down the lawless movement' by taking action under the Trespass Act of 1865. Nor did they use the police to charge the raiders with taking illegal possession of land as had happened under the previous government in 1902. Lady Cathcart played down the significance of the raid, claiming that it was a demonstration organised by young men and boys, encouraged by newspaper reporters.[20]

At this time it was reported that Donald MacDonald was 'mentally incapable' and that his son, Archibald, was in control of the farm. The cottars did not have any contact with the MacDonalds or their workers. The cottars were said not to be amenable to listening to advice, their patience being exhausted, although another report described Duncan Campbell as 'civil and open to reasoning.' Campbell was reported to have said that the cottars would not seize or survey any part of Vatersay Farm until after Martinmas term (11 November), thus contradicting his threat to MacDonald in December, but he did not keep this undertaking. The Rev. William MacKenzie of Craigston, Barra, was said to be in sympathy with the cottars. The Catholic priests were supportive throughout the raiding and settlement, which was vital to the raiders, as the priests were such important figures.[21]

So, by the spring of 1906, the cottars had carried out raids on Vatersay almost annually since 1900. They had marked out symbolic crofts for themselves, but the only concrete result of

1. (*Above*) View of Castle Bay, Barra, and the islands to the south. Beyond the two eastern arms of Vatersay are Sandray (on the left), then Pabbay, Mingulay (the highest) and Berneray (1991).

2. (*Left*) Lady Gordon Cathcart, owner of Vatersay at the time of the raids. By Chevalier L Desanges, 1867.

3. The herring curing station on the south shore of Bàgh Bhatarsaigh in the 1870s. It operated from the 1860s to 1892.

Vatersay, Barra, from the East

4. The eastern end of the herring station, a postcard based on a photograph taken at the same time as above.

5. The raiders' huts on the site of the present township of Vatersay, in September 1908. Beyond are the fields of Vatersay Farm.

6. As above, looking towards Barra. In the centre are the remains of the stone buildings of the farm steading.

7. The ten Vatersay raiders, with their two legal advisers (back left and back right), before their trial in Edinburgh on 2 June 1908. See Appendix 1 for names.

8. Vatersay Township in 1927. Vatersay House stands on the left of the crofting strips on the hill.

9. Vatersay House (left) and Township in 1948. (*Alasdair Alpin MacGregor*)

10. The eastern part of Vatersay Township in 1949, looking towards Bàgh Siar. Most of the houses on the right were demolished in 1975 when bungalows were built there (seen on the right of the picture below).

11. Vatersay Township in 2006, from the same viewpoint as plate 5. The wooden council bungalows were built in 1975-6, and most of the other houses were built or renovated after the opening of the causeway.

12. The ruins of Vatersay House, 2006. Built in the eighteenth century, its last long-term inhabitant left in 1909.

13. Bringing home the hay across the machair in 1948. Left to right: Donald John MacLeod, Anthony MacNeil, Margaret MacLeod, William –, Catherine MacLeod, Hector MacLeod. (*Alasdair Alpin MacGregor*)

14. Nan MacKinnon, who was celebrated for her knowledge of Gaelic oral tradition.

15. Donald Campbell ("Thomson"), postman, at Uidh in 1952. The church is on the left.

16. The Church of Our Lady of the Waves and St John, built in 1913, photographed in about 1950.

17. The interior of the church as it was originally, photographed in 1981. The altar rail came from St Columba's Chapel, Mingulay.

18. The pupils and staff of Vatersay School in about 1935. See Appendix 6 for names.

19. Vatersay School and Schoolhouse. Built in 1927, the school closed in 1994 and was still disused when this photograph was taken in 1998.

20. A puffer on the beach of Bàgh Bhatarsaigh. These flat-bottomed boats were grounded at high tide and their cargo, such as coal, was then unloaded. The 1927 school is on the left.

21. Caraigrigh, Uidh, from Creag Mhòr, in 1998. The renovated house right of centre was originally built by Hector MacKinnon in 1911.

22. Peggy MacLean (Bean Bharnaidh) spinning in her house at 2 Caolas in 1927. The MacLeans came from Mingulay. (*Alasdair Alpin MacGregor*)

23. Caolas in 1948. Beyond is Bentangaval, the southern extremity of Barra, and, far right, Sheabhal on Barra. (*Alasdair Alpin MacGregor*)

24. The first car ferry to Vatersay delivering a mobile shop to the slipway at Caolas in August 1975 when the service began.

25. Maggie, James and Flora Gillies stacking hay at 15 Caolas in the 1940s.

26. The causeway linking Vatersay (right) and Barra. It was completed in 1991. (2006)

27. Eorasdail in 1948. The settlement was the most remote of the four townships created in 1909, and was deserted in about 1965. (*Alasdair Alpin MacGregor*)

28. The township of Eorasdail in 2006. The three small freestanding stone structures were the fireplaces of wooden houses. Beyond is the island of Muldoanich.

29. Mingulay Village in decay in August 1909. Most of the people had already left for Vatersay by this time. The large building is the Chapel House.

30. Houses in Mingulay in August 1909. The half-hidden house belonged to Michael MacNeil, the last to leave Mingulay in 1912.

31. Sarah MacShane, teacher at Mingulay School, and her remaining pupils outside the schoolhouse in August 1909. The three children closest to her are her own. They all transferred to Vatersay School in June 1910.

32. The scant remains of the shepherd's house east of Bàgh Bàn, Sandray. Shepherds lived there from 1835, when the Sandray people were evicted, until 1904. (1991)

33. The Sandray raiders, who were all from Mingulay, at Sheader in October 1909. Most of this group are members of the family of John Gillies.

34. Neil, Maggie and Flora Gillies at Sheader, October 1909.
Vatersay is in the distance.

their direct action was the purchase and renting by the Congested Districts Board of two areas of land for growing potatoes. They were no nearer their ultimate goal, which was to have crofts on the island. Their next step was to be more decisive.

5. The invasion, 1906–1907

On 27 June 1906 Mr Garson, of Lady Cathcart's solicitors, the firm Skene, Edwards and Garson, Edinburgh, wrote to Reginald MacLeod, Under-Secretary at the Scottish Office, reporting that:

Some of the cottars had taken cattle over in boats and had put them on lands in the occupation of the farm tenant. The factor saw Mr Duncan Campbell, who is understood to be the mouthpiece of the cottars, but he could not get any information as to the people to whom the cattle belonged. Mr Campbell informed him that it is the intention of the cottars to put more cattle on Vatersay this week. The tenant of Vatersay is very seriously concerned, and is afraid to take any step for his own protection in case of injury being done to his stock by the cottars. We think that if the government were to cause intimation to be made locally, that these high-handed proceedings would not be tolerated, the cottars would probably remove their stock quietly. Unless something is done promptly and vigorously the situation is pretty certain to be very seriously aggravated . . . We shall be very much obliged if you will let us know that we can count on such protection being given as was stipulated for by the tenant when he agreed . . . in the matter of giving potato ground to the cottars.[1]

MacLeod's curt reply was that it was the landlord's responsibility to deal with the situation. On another occasion he expressed the view that the conciliatory way in which the Congested Districts Board dealt with lawlessness merely encouraged it. Nothing was done, promptly or vigorously, and the situation developed as predicted. More cattle were taken over, including a heifer belonging to Duncan Campbell who informed the Castlebay police of his intention to do so.[2]

John Wilson, Sheriff of Inverness-shire, wrote to MacLeod on 5 July:

The chief constable suggests that the whole matter is one for the civil courts, and that the proprietor and tenant should take such proceedings as they think proper. I think, however, that the best course is to get the local inspector of police to suggest to the men that they should remove the cattle . . . if they do so, that would obviate proceedings which otherwise Lady Cathcart may take to obtain a warrant to remove and sell the cattle to defray expenses. Mr Garson is most anxious to avoid the necessity for any legal proceedings which might be the means of accentuating feeling and creating further disturbance in the islands, and he agreed 1) not to take proceedings in the meantime, and 2) to allow the cottars to remove the cattle without exacting any claim for damage done.[3]

Again, the government took no action, and if the police did 'suggest' to the men that they remove their cattle, they took no notice. Some of the cattle which the factor referred to were, according to a writer in *The Scotsman* nearly three years later (26 February 1909) very likely owned by 'merchants and prosperous crofters in Barra. The raiders desired to make as strong a show as possible when they took possession of the island, and they were assisted to that end by Barra merchants, who practically used the raiders as instruments for their own advantage.' In other words, the merchants were getting free grazing.

On 28 July the cattle were followed by their owners or minders to Vatersay. This was the most significant raid yet, for the forty raiders, crowded into two boats, not only selected house sites around the old farm steading, but some started to make preparations to stay. The raid was significant also because it was the first in which men from Mingulay took part. They were Donald MacPhee, John Sinclair and Hugh MacLean, part of the crew of the *Snowbird*, owned by MacPhee. PC MacMaster dutifully reported the events of the day – momentous in retrospect – which he himself was unaware of until he saw boats returning from Vatersay to Castlebay that evening. Duncan Campbell had informed him: 'Each of the men marked off a site for himself by cutting off a small sod and driving a wooden peg into the ground, that afterwards they started to build up the walls of the old farm steading, the greater part of which had fallen, which they intend to roof and occupy as temporary dwellings till they get other houses erected. Donald

MacDonald, farmer, informed me that he saw the men at work from his sitting room window but that he did not go near them.'

There is a story that one of the raiders completed building a dwelling and had a fire lit in it in one day, which entitled him, under an old law, to remain in occupation of the house. There is such a law, but no mention of this has been found in any of the reports at the time or in the following years, so it is uncertain. The reports indicate that in those first few days, and perhaps for longer, the cottars returned to Barra in the evenings. They did not seem to be in any particular hurry to establish themselves or 'to make as strong a show as possible' with their own presence as they had done with the cattle.

The following day, Campbell again acted as informant for MacMaster:

> At a meeting of cottars held at Castlebay Roman Catholic Chapel at the close of the forenoon service it was resolved that the cottars were to go again to Vatersay today to continue building up the old steading walls, that several of the cottars appealed against settling at Vatersay steading, saying that they preferred Caolas, that it was decided that they should go there tomorrow to select sites for houses, and that he expected eight or ten of them to go there.

Twenty six went to the steading, and ten to Caolas; all were Barra cottars. Mingulay men are not recorded as taking part again for some months. The steading formed a rough square of barns and byres at the bottom of the slope on which Vatersay House stands. The southernmost houses of the township of Vatersay are roughly on the site of the west side of the steading. The road past these houses was a road of sorts then, and on the other (east) side of it were two or three buildings (see plate 6 and map 3).

Two days after the raid, Donald MacDonald put up notices in the Castlebay area saying that he had rounded up the cottars' cattle and horses and would only release them on payment of a fee for each one. PC MacMaster reported:

Shortly afterwards a number of the cottars gathered at the pier and started discussing the matter in a pretty excited manner. Seventeen of the cottars left for Vatersay and another boat load left from Kentangaval . . . at 8pm the cottars returned and their leader, Duncan Campbell, informed me that he found the cattle and horses in separate pens at Vatersay farm steading, that he asked Mr MacDonald to release them, but he refused to do so unless they (the cottars) paid him 10/- a head for the cattle and 12/- for the horses, for their upkeep during the time they were grazing at the farm, that he (Campbell) opened the gates of both pens and assisted by the cottars drove the cattle to that part of Vatersay known as Earsdale [Eorasdail] and left them there to graze.

By 9 August five huts, including wooden and stone-built types, had been started; Roderick MacLean, a merchant from Glen was the first named builder of a hut, although it took him a long time to complete it. The rebuilt walls of the steading had been knocked down by Donald MacDonald.[4]

Mingulay was mentioned again on 2 August when Michael Campbell (nick-named 'Teic'), who was a prominent member of the community and described as the leader of the raiders from

Mingulay, attempted to build a hut at Ledag, on the east side of Castlebay. He stopped when asked to by the Garrygall crofters. He had relatives there, which probably explains why he chose to build there instead of Vatersay. Perhaps he was unsure about joining in with the Barra men; he may have felt different being from Mingulay. The Mingulay people were regarded in Barra as being self-contained and a little reserved.[5]

The Mingulay people must have been inspired to think about their own lot by the raids on Vatersay over the previous six years. Mingulay is ten kilometres (six miles) south of Vatersay, and fifteen kilometres (nine miles) from Barra, and the sea is treacherous, with fickle currents between the islands. On top of that, Mingulay had no sheltered harbour or landing place, and boats had to be landed on, and launched from, the exposed beach. The people could be cut off for weeks on end, and a visitor in 1897 claimed that it was easier to get to America than to Mingulay. The island was 'congested' in the language of the time, having a large number of cottars – families without crofts – and too many people in general. There had been a large influx of people evicted from other islands in the 1830s, and the population continued to grow, becoming too high for the island to support. The village became overcrowded and there were outbreaks of diseases such as typhoid and measles. The population in 1901 was 135, down from a peak of about 160 in the 1880s.

In the later nineteenth century the people of Mingulay tried to supplement their traditional economy based on crofting, fishing and fowling for seabirds by getting involved in the developing fishing industry based in Castlebay, but they were hampered by their remoteness and the lack of a harbour and landing place. These drawbacks also made it harder to land supplies at a time when the people were becoming more dependent on the outside world for food and other essentials. The visitor in 1897 said that 'it is no unusual occurrence for them to have to throw their bags of meal into the sea and drag them ashore by means of a rope.' Getting the doctor or, just as important, the priest, from Barra in an emergency was often impossible. Education, from 1859, and travelling to other parts of the country for fishing and other work, would have opened their eyes to the living standards and ways of the outside world. Education also gave them the ability and confidence to call for improvements to the landing facilities and, eventually, new land on Vatersay. In 1883 a few families moved to newly created holdings in Garrygall in Barra.

In 1896 the islanders appealed to the Secretary for Scotland to help them in constructing a 'boat-slip with boat-hauling convenience.' It took the form of a petition signed by the men of the island, and called 'the cry of a sorely distressed community'. The Congested Districts Board took on the project, and in 1901 installed a derrick for winching supplies out of boats, rather than, as originally intended, for winching boats themselves out of the sea. The derrick may have been useful, but it did not solve the problem of what to do with the boats. It must have been a disappointment and, coupled with the Barra men's raids on Vatersay, added to the case for evacuation.

Photographs taken on Mingulay in 1905 show some signs of prosperity in that many of the thatched houses had been improved with glazed windows and chimneys. There were also two houses built in modern style with gables and felt roofs. One of these, in the village, had been built before 1901; the other, south of the village near the school, was built after 1901, perhaps several years after. Clearly their builders had no thoughts of leaving in the near future. Some of the fishermen were doing well: by 1894 two of them had acquired large herring fishing boats, which they kept at Castlebay as they were too big to beach at Mingulay. A factor in the apparent prosperity could have been the effect of the Crofters Act of 1886 which gave crofters security of tenure and thus an incentive to improve their houses. A fine Roman Catholic chapel had been built in 1898, financed by a Castlebay merchant. But Roderick MacNeil, interviewed in 1960, said there had been talk of evacuation long before it started. In the autumn of 1905 Morag Campbell Finlayson wrote of the coming winter 'we shall be like prisoners in the bad weather . . . I am hoping to leave Mingulay soon.' Two months later she had moved to Kentangaval. The 1905 photographs show that at least two houses had been deserted.[6]

The building of huts on Vatersay continued throughout the autumn of 1906. Duncan Campbell transferred his hut from Kentangaval in October, and moved in a month later. This was the third hut to be completed. Roderick MacNeil from Horve, Castlebay, had been the first to complete his and take up residence, and Roderick MacLean had completed but not moved into a hut. All three huts were near the farm steading. Also in November, Michael Campbell and his nephew, Duncan Sinclair from Mingulay, began building the 30-foot (nine metre) long hut Campbell had attempted to build at Ledag in August. Campbell, his widowed sister, Catherine Sinclair, Duncan and other men from Mingulay took up residence in January 1907, the pioneers in the escape from the struggle for survival in Mingulay. At about this time an official of the Board wrote, 'this is not trespass under pressure of poverty but an elaborate scheme of invasion.'

The stand-off between the farmer and the raiders also continued. In October 1906 he instructed his workers to round up all the raiders' cattle and horses and ferry them over the sound to Bentangaval, Barra. The same afternoon their owners brought them back again and the following day the farce was repeated. There were 'hot words' between Duncan Campbell and John MacDonald, the factor, over the dispute. By the end of December the raiders had transferred their cattle to the Board's former potato ground at Creag Mhòr.[7]

Apart from appeals and warnings from the factor, no action was taken against the raiders until April 1907. Lady Cathcart's agents, having failed to persuade the government to do anything, initiated legal proceedings against thirteen raiders, requiring them to leave. Interim interdicts (injunctions) were granted in the Court of Session in Edinburgh and a messenger-at-arms was despatched to serve them on 8 April, but he only found eleven of the thirteen. The thirteen were presumably those who had built thirteen huts – although some huts were built and occupied by many people – and dug thirteen potato plots in an enclosure north of the farmhouse. Raiders who had built dwellings elsewhere by then, such as at Caolas, were not interdicted, nor were any of the women who had arrived by then, presumably because the men they were with were regarded as the heads of households. Women are all but invisible in the records and newspaper accounts – which was normal for the time – but it was their determination as much as the men's which led to the raiding and settlement of Vatersay. The raiders were also supported in their cause by the Castlebay priest, Father Donald Martin.

Six of the eleven were from Barra: Duncan Campbell (Donnchadh Antonaidh), from Kentangaval; Donald MacIntyre (Dòmhnall Mhicheil Dubh) John Campbell (Iagan Mhicheil), William Boyd (Uilleam Boid), all from Garrygall; Roderick MacNeil (Ruairidh Iain), from Castlebay; and John MacDougall (Iain Raghnaill), from Glen. Five were from Mingulay: Michael Campbell (Teic); his nephew, Duncan Sinclair (Donnchadh Anndra Dhonnchaidh); Duncan's cousin, John Sinclair (Iagan Iain Dhonnchaidh), and the brothers Hector and Neil MacPhee (Eachann & Niall Dhòmhnaill). All were described as fishermen, apart from Boyd and MacDougall, for whom no occupations were given. The Mingulay men, like the Barra men, were all cottars, but Mingulay crofters also started to leave; as we have seen, remoteness and inaccessibility as well as landlessness were the main reasons for leaving Mingulay.

The court records continue: 'The respondents have entirely disregarded the interdict, and have continued to trespass upon the farm . . . and have interfered with the petitioner and her tenant in the peaceable possession and enjoyment of the said farm.' Details of breaches were given; they were seen planting potatoes, and building or roofing huts, in the case of Boyd, this was a stone hut at Gortein near where the school was later built.[8]

The serving of the interdicts was mentioned by John Mac-Dougall in the only known detailed account of an aspect of the raids by a raider, recorded on tape in 1960. It is given here in full:

I was living in Glen at that time. I had no land but my father had a croft. There were many more people living in Castlebay and round about it at that time than there are today. There was fishing and people were at the fishing, myself included. The world wasn't like it is now – you couldn't just run down to get 'assistance' [benefits] – it was a matter of if you can't help yourself to survive you die.

There were meetings and talk and planning . . . who wants some land . . . if you were married and had a family to raise, a bit of land was useful. Domhnall Bhatarsach [Donald MacDonald, the farmer] gave land in Uidh for people to grow some potatoes on. I myself used to go over there before I married. But that wasn't much. You had to cross over in a boat and you couldn't plant as much as you wished.

There were a number of sheds in Vatersay village when I went over there [in 1907]. Although I erected a shed in Vatersay, I didn't go to live there, but I intended to go there. Then, one day when I was landing some wood on the island, for someone else, this little man came along with an interdict for me . . . I didn't take it from him at first . . . when he jumped into the boat, I would jump out! Then, I said to myself, 'Ach, I might as well . . .' He gave me this piece of paper which said that I was breaking the law.[9]

MacDougall applied for and got a croft at Uidh in 1909, but after two of his daughters had died as infants in Vatersay, he and his wife returned to Barra.

In May 1907 John Wilson, Sheriff of Inverness-shire, went to Vatersay at the request of John Sinclair, Secretary for Scotland, to attempt to persuade the raiders to leave. He was escorted to and around Vatersay by Duncan Campbell, who gave Wilson 'full information as to himself and his views . . . he is a fisherman, 50 years of age, somewhat lame, with four sons and two daughters . . . for 12 or 13 years prior to 1906 he lived in Kentangaval in the wooden hut now occupied by him on Vatersay . . . the site of the hut was unhealthy and his wife and family suffered ill-health.' Campbell invited Wilson into his hut, where he met Mrs Campbell, 'a most respectable-looking woman,' who was, incidentally, originally from Mingulay.

Wilson met several other raiders. One of these was Neil MacPhee from Mingulay who was building a hut, the fourteenth wooden hut, near the farm steading. MacPhee complained of the remoteness of Mingulay, the lack of land for a croft or house of his own, and the lack of seaweed for fertiliser which compelled him to bring fish-guts for the purpose from Castlebay, during the fishing season when time was most precious. Both his parents had died of typhoid in Mingulay in 1894. He said that he 'had grown sick of waiting and would prefer imprisonment rather than go back to Mingulay to starve or be driven to the United States.' MacPhee had been interdicted but the case against him was dropped before the trial, possibly due to a clerical error. William Boyd, who had begun building a house without permission at Garrygall, Barra, the previous December, had received a letter from the factor warning him that 'if you persist in building, the erection will be pulled down forcibly, or Lady Cathcart's agents will take immediate action against you.' Roderick MacNeil's hut in Castlebay was built over a stream near a fish-curing station, and 'in the fishing months the smell of rotting fish-refuse was sickening.'

Wilson described the raiders he met as 'respectable men, and except in their views as to their right to get land and to take it if need be, they appeared to me to be both intelligent and reasonable . . . courteous and kindly. They were most anxious to do as little harm as possible to the tenant of the farm.'

The raiders pointed out their historical claim to Vatersay: 'Up to 50 years ago their grandparents and remoter ancestors had had crofts on Vatersay at the very place where the raiders' huts were now set up, and though their grandparents had been evicted, their descendants had never given up their claim. These descendants down to this day have continued to bury their dead on Vatersay.' Duncan Campbell had put his hut on the actual site of the house of his grandparents James Campbell and Kirsty Mac-Neil.

Sheriff Wilson failed to persuade the raiders to abandon their 'illegal conduct'. He concluded:

It seemed to me that there were influences at work which were not fully disclosed . . . Their firm conviction was that Lady Cathcart would not be a party to imprisoning them or evicting them; further, that the government would not allow them to suffer. From time to time one or other of the men vowed that he would suffer imprisonment or death rather than yield . . . if they were put down, scores of others would take up the struggle. There seems to be a considerable body of local opinion to the effect that Lady Cathcart has not fully appreciated her duty as landowner, and that long indifference to the necessities of the cottars has gone far to drive them to exasperation.

Wilson foresaw two possible outcomes of the Vatersay situation. One was for Lady Cathcart to proceed with her legal action, which, if it resulted in imprisonment of the raiders, may lead to 'serious disturbance'. The second was for the government to buy all or part of Vatersay for crofting use. His report, giving the raiders' viewpoint and hardly mentioning the factor's or the farmer's, gave the impression that he was sympathetic to the raiders, and it was therefore criticised by Lady Cathcart and her agents.[10]

Lady Cathcart was further enraged in August 1907 when the Lord Advocate, Thomas Shaw, played down the seriousness of the Vatersay situation in a statement during a debate in the House of Commons which she rightly regarded as highly provocative. Having said of his own position, 'It rests on me to maintain order in Scotland,' he went on to say of the raiders, 'these poor things stepped across to the island of Vatersay and on the shore they planted a few potatoes, hoping to return in the spring to reap what little harvest there was . . . they were interfering with no human soul', and he implied that the land was a 'barren waste'. This incredible condoning of law-breakers would come to haunt the government, for it could hardly have been more encouraging to the raiders of Vatersay and of other land in the Hebrides. He also referred to her as a 'proprietor who had been unfortunate in his [sic] relations with his tenants.' Shaw said he did not want to 'repeat the sad history of events which preceded the Crofters' Act', referring to the heavy-handed response to crofters and cottars standing up to oppressive landlords.[11]

Sinclair and Shaw were condemned by Arthur Balfour, the leader of the opposition (and previous Conservative Prime

Minister), who said that 'they had looked on with indifference while the law was being grossly violated; that they had permitted serious personal loss to be inflicted upon a proprietor and a tenant-farmer; that "they had behaved outrageously to the one" and with harsh inconsideration to the other.'[12]

Relations between the estate and the new Liberal government were already strained by the latter's land reform proposals in favour of small-holders. The reforms were intended to improve on the Crofters Act of 1886 by enabling the creation of new crofts, if necessary by an element of compulsion on proprietors. The policy was that of 'dual ownership', whereby crofters would be tenants of proprietors, rather than purchasers of crofts on land purchased by the Congested Districts Board, as had been the policy of the previous Conservative government. This had happened in the case of Northbay Farm in Barra in 1901, but the crofters later appealed, successfully, to become tenants. In the case of the estate of Kilmuir, Skye, bought by the Board in 1904, prospective crofters refused to cooperate with the Board's proposals that they buy their crofts, and the Board had to back down.

Lady Cathcart's agents had condemned the Secretary for Scotland, John Sinclair, as 'a man with no administrative experience' and the Lord Advocate as 'an extreme radical' and 'hostile to landowners'. They were right about Shaw, who had defended the raiders of the Pairc deer forest in Lewis, from which their forebears had been evicted, in 1888. Sinclair proposed that Lady Cathcart should 'clear up the doubts which seem to exist as to the water resources of Vatersay' and then create crofts on the island, with the usual financial and practical assistance from the

Congested Districts Board. In view of Lady Cathcart's bad feelings towards the government, he felt it wise to reassure her (in a letter written by the under-secretary, Reginald MacLeod) that he was 'well aware that the Vatersay situation is trying for everybody involved, for none more so than the proprietor. He regrets greatly to think of her anxieties.' A hint of sarcasm perhaps from a man whose sympathies were well known to lie with the other side.[13]

Lady Cathcart refused to turn Vatersay into a crofting settlement, on five principal grounds. First, as she had stated many times before, she had broken up all her farms in Barra for crofting use, but she maintained that some of the crofting schemes had not been a success. Second, because of her experience of other islands, such as Mingulay, where many tenants had not paid rent for years, she was not in principle in favour of creating another crofting settlement on an island. Third, she was advised that the island's water supply was not sufficient for large numbers of crofting tenants, and there were also no proper landing places or roads, and no church or school. Fourth, she did not regard the raiders who had taken 'violent possession', in her words, of her property as suitable tenants. Fifth, she said the government was responsible for compensating the tenant farmer for giving up his lease which he had only recently renewed. There were other factors: one was that the burden of rates for providing a water supply and school would fall on her as proprietor; another, that a farm in South Uist (South Glendale) which she had agreed to break up for crofting turned out to be suitable for only a few crofts. She said that the government should either put down the 'lawless movement' or purchase the whole farm and make terms with the tenant farmer.[14]

Although she had created crofts in Barra since becoming proprietor in 1878, and had sold land to the Congested Districts Board for crofting, Lady Cathcart was criticised in various quarters for resisting demands for new crofts on her South Uist estate, and for the consequent number of cottars. She claimed that 'it has always been my earnest and anxious wish to act sympathetically towards the inhabitants of these western islands and I have tried to go upon the lines (which I venture to think is the highest form of charity) of helping them to rise into positions whereby they can help themselves . . . I have often been discouraged by public misrepresentations of my actings and motives.' Lady Cathcart had helped individuals with loans for fishing boats and gear, and provided bursaries for promising young men to continue their education and training. In many ways she was not a bad landlord, but she tends to be remembered for the negative or unpopular aspects of her proprietorship. She was held in some respect by the people, but, as the raiders pointed out, she did not have a good understanding of current conditions on her estate, not having visited it since 1878. She thought otherwise: this lady of the landed gentry, owner of vast estates and opulent residences in Scotland and England, instructed her solicitors to make the extraordinary claim regarding the raiding of Vatersay, that she was 'intimately acquainted with the local conditions and the influences that have been in operation.'[15]

Sinclair declined the offer to buy the island, saying it would be against the government's stated policy of assisting private land-owners in creating new crofts. Sinclair also said it was not known at this stage whether the whole island would be needed for a crofting settlement, and he regarded the issue of compensation to the tenant as a matter for the proprietor. He later admitted he was using the Vatersay case as a test for his proposed land reform bill which had already been blocked in 1906 and 1907 by the House of Lords. Had it succeeded, he might have had a stronger hand in his dealings with Lady Cathcart. He also admitted, confidentially to the Lord Advocate, that 'ultimately purchase may be forced upon us.'

In October 1907 Lady Cathcart finally agreed to do as the government wished, on certain conditions, and there followed months of correspondence between the two sides as to the terms of the proposals. In one of these exchanges, Lady Cathcart's agents dishonestly maintained that the tenant's lease had been signed (in August 1906) before the raiders began settling; the case for compensation to the tenant would thus appear stronger than if he had signed after the settlement began. Sinclair knew the facts, which, he maintained, absolved the government of any obligation to pay compensation.[16]

By October twenty-two huts had been built; clearly the legal action against the raiders had not been a deterrent to further raiding. Lady Cathcart's agents said that 'the people believe that they have the support of the government in their action, and it is obvious that they are being advised from the outside, as when threatened with proceedings for breach of interdict they have stated that they cannot be prosecuted without the consent of the Lord Advocate, and that the Lord Advocate will not give his consent.' The people were encouraged by the success of the crofters of Kilmuir, Skye, in standing up to their landlord, in this case the Board, which had bought the estate in 1904; they refused to cooperate with the Board's proposals for them to buy their crofts. Their perseverance – in turn encouraged by their Vatersay counterparts (albeit with a different landlord) – paid off in May 1908 when the Board agreed to them being tenants.

Of the twenty-two huts, twelve had been built by Barra families, and nine by Mingulay families. These nine represented about a third of Mingulay's population. In June, John MacLean (Barnaidh) of Mingulay had stated in a letter to the Congested Districts Board that 'my neighbours are all leaving this island for settlement at Vatersay.' He had applied to rent the Board's potato ground at Creag Mhòr to use for grazing, but the Board declined the request. One hut had been built by the family of John Campbell, including two children and three grandchildren, from Pabbay. The three families on Pabbay had led a precarious existence since the loss of four of their men (and a man from Barra) in a storm while fishing ten years earlier. Although conditions for landing boats were better than on Mingulay, and there was some good land, life must have been particularly hard with very few men left to man a boat. Seeing their Mingulay neighbours and relatives leaving, the Campbells also seized the opportunity to leave. By February 1908 a further nine huts had been built on Vatersay, and very few were built subsequently, so the majority of the settlers arrived during 1907.[17]

On 19 November 1907 the police constable at Castlebay reported the news that Sandray had also been raided. Six Mingulay men, showing a certain independence of spirit in not joining their kinsmen on Vatersay, landed at Sheader on the west coast, where people had lived before the whole population was evicted in about 1835. Since then the island had been used as grazing by Vatersay Farm, inhabited only by a shepherd living at Bàgh Bàn on the north east coast. Donald MacMillan, the shepherd for several decades, had died in 1904, and had not been replaced. The raiders, some of them descended from the former inhabitants, proceeded to build houses of stone and thatch, using stones from the ruins of earlier dwellings, and by the beginning of January 1908 they had completed and moved into two houses. They were John Gillies, his brother-in-law, John MacNeil (who was not only Gillies's sister's husband but also his wife's brother), Donald MacNeil, John Mac-Lean (Barnaidh), John MacKinnon and Michael MacNeil (an Righ, 'The King', a nickname, not a reference to his status!). In the spring they brought cattle over, and planted potatoes. They carried on lobster fishing, which was easier there than from Mingulay, as there was a good sheltered beach for landing on, they got better bait there, and Castlebay, where they sold the lobsters, was much nearer.[18]

By the end of 1907, therefore, most of the people who were to settle illegally on Vatersay had arrived, and Sandray had also been raided. It was hardly 'an elaborate scheme of invasion' as a Board official called it, there being no apparent scheme after the initial show of strength on 28 July 1906. No-one at that time could have foreseen how the raiding would develop, or that most of the population of Mingulay would decamp to Vatersay. Meanwhile Lady Cathcart and the Scottish Office were engaged in a long wrangle over various issues. She tried but failed to persuade the Scottish Office to take action against the raiders, for which it was widely criticised – the failure to act was seen as tacit support for the raiders not only of Vatersay, but of farms in other islands.

She therefore initiated legal proceedings against some of the raiders. The Scottish Office also declined to buy the island, claiming this would be against government policy, and the two sides could not agree on the terms under which Lady Cathcart would create a crofting settlement.

6. The trial, 1908

In January 1908 Lady Cathcart served a complaint for breach of interdict and contempt of court on eleven raiders, requiring them to leave (the number was later reduced to ten, when the case against Neil MacPhee was dropped, possibly due to a clerical error). As related in the Prologue, she had suspended her legal action in order to give the raiders the opportunity to obey the interim interdicts and leave, and while she was negotiating with the Congested Districts Board over the terms of the proposed crofting settlement on Vatersay.[1] 'They could not obey the order of the court,' reported *The Glasgow Herald* of 19 February, 'because they had no other place to go. They had no money to take them elsewhere. They had no food for themselves or their dependants apart from the potatoes which they grew and milk from the cattle which grazed on the land.'

The invasion of Vatersay had continued unabated, and by February 1908, thirty-one families were resident. At about this time one of the three or so families on Berneray, that of Donald Campbell, decided that they, too, would take the opportunity to leave. Berneray, also known as Barra Head, is the most remote of the Barra Isles, and the most southerly of the Outer Hebrides. Life there was particularly tough because of the island's remoteness and lack of fertile land, although it did have a landing place and other facilities built for the lighthouse in the 1830s.[2]

At about this time the raiders began a lively correspondence with politicians and other influential people whose support might be enlisted, or to harangue those – such as members of the House of Lords – who had spoken out against the raiders. The House of Lords was highly unpopular in crofting areas because of its consistent blocking of Scottish Secretary John Sinclair's land reform proposals, which was hardly surprising since many of their Lordships were themselves landowners whose interests would be adversely affected by the proposed reforms. In a letter to Lord Balfour of Burleigh, a former Scottish Secretary who had facilitated the purchase of land in northern Barra for crofting in 1901, the raiders stated 'our most earnest desire is that your Lordship may live to see the downfall of the House of Lords.'[3] The raids in the region as a whole were partly a response to the blocking tactics of the Lords.

The eloquent, articulate and sometimes cheeky letters were written by Neil MacPhee of Mingulay, Niall Chaluim, not to be confused with his younger cousin, also from Mingulay, of the same name – Niall Dhòmhnaill – who was interdicted. Niall Chaluim was a man of remarkable ability considering the modest educational opportunities he had had. His formal education at Mingulay School up to the age of fourteen was the same as that of his contemporaries, yet some of these could not even sign their names. His astonishing breadth of knowledge, and grasp of politics – and of English, a second language to him – show that he was well read and he must have read newspapers regularly. He followed the on-going debates on the land question at Westminster from 1906 onwards, and he was well versed in crofting legislation. He must have been well aware of other cases of land raids. He was known as 'the scholar' locally and was described as 'Duncan Campbell's right hand man, troublesome fellow' by an official of the Congested Districts Board. Whether he had been involved in 'agitation' before is not known. He was not among the early raiders; he probably moved to Vatersay with his mother and sisters after his father died in Mingulay in January 1908, which ties in with the beginning of the correspondence. He was thirty three at the time.[4]

Meanwhile the case was attracting interest from the press, and was debated in both houses of Parliament. A writer in *The Glasgow Herald* of 1 April 1908 commented: 'With the admission before us of an extraordinary proceeding there is no avoiding the conclusion that the Scotch Office and the government have been landed by Vatersay in a bog . . . the Scotch Office approached Lady Cathcart's complaint so surcharged with tenderness for the alleged culprits as to blind them to the injustice of letting lawlessness enjoy even the briefest triumph.'

This was the view of the Conservative opposition, which naturally sympathised with the landowner. *The Scotsman* of 17 April 1908 drew parallels with a case in Lewis in 1891, when raiders occupied the farm of Orinsay. They rebuilt old houses and cultivated the land, claiming descent from crofters who had been evicted from the land fifty years before. The landowner took them to court under the Trespass Act of 1865 (under the

terms of the Act, the prosecution had to be raised by the Crown,
in the form of the Procurator Fiscal), and they were sentenced to
the maximum jail term, fourteen days. This would seem to have
been a valid precedent for using the Act against the Vatersay
raiders, but Sinclair and Lord Advocate Thomas Shaw went to
great lengths to deny this. They claimed the case was a matter of
civil law, to be pursued by the proprietor, rather than of criminal
law. The previous Conservative government had used the police
to charge raiders of Vatersay in 1902 with taking illegal possession of land, but Sinclair did not adopt this course.[5]

As related in the Prologue, the raiders were sentenced to two
months imprisonment for breach of interdict and contempt of
court, not for the original crime of illegally occupying land. The
trial aroused enormous public interest and sympathy, even out-
rage. People were intrigued by the trial and imprisonment in
Edinburgh of ten humble fishermen from the remote and little
known Outer Hebrides. Petitions for their release were sent by
trades councils, Liberal Associations and ordinary citizens from all
over Scotland, including one from Barra, written by Neil
MacPhee. A relief fund for the men's families was launched
by *The Edinburgh Evening News*, which reached £174 by the time
of their release. A key figure in this groundswell of support was
their solicitor, Donald Shaw. He must have been at least partly
responsible for getting 300 sympathisers to welcome the raiders
to Edinburgh. His desire to provide cabs in preference to the
prison van shows how anxious he and his 'welcome committee'
were that the raiders were not treated or regarded as common
criminals. Another illustration of this was shown when, at some
point before the trial, press photographers took photographs of

the raiders, who were dressed in suits for the occasion. These suits must have been hired or borrowed by the committee, since in court, and on their release from prison, they were dressed in their blue fishing clothes. It is strange that since they had the suits on the morning of the trial, they did not wear them in court.[6]

The case fuelled the on-going debate about the land question and the failure of the Crofters' Act of 1886 to provide for the creation of new crofts, resulting in growing numbers of cottars. It revived memories of earlier land raids and other cases going back to the 1880s where tenants stood up to oppressive landlords in the Hebrides, and there were pitched battles between raiders and police (or soldiers in gunboats) sent to clear them off the land they had raided. *The Glasgow Herald* of 18 July 1908 felt it necessary to correct misconceptions about the raiders:

An impression has got abroad that the Barra raider is a fiercely rebellious fellow. As a matter of fact, he is rather phlegmatic. He is surely the mildest mannered person who ever set a country's laws at defiance. His gentle blue eyes (the children of these islands have eyes of the gentlest blue like the colour of the waters that in sunny mood lap the rocky fringe of their island home) suggest a nature slow to revolt. The waters are not always placid. The genial blue changes suddenly and often to surly green and the sea turns in wrath . . . the raiders of Barra have not in them the stuff of the true rebel . . . the talk of gunboats in these waters or a force of Glasgow policemen on the islands to protect the interests of landlordism may be dismissed as the idlest of rhetoric.

Still, the islanders, if slow in wrath, are resolute of purpose. The most striking feature of their raids is the calm deliberation with which they were accomplished. Nor were they undertaken without reckoning the cost. They have been described as an 'ignorant people', a description singularly inapt, as inapt as the term 'poor things' applied to them by the learned Lord Advocate, though poor in worldly possessions many of them may be. On the contrary they are a wonderfully shrewd, a reflective and a prescient people. The men who led the raiders to Vatersay were fully conscious of their action . . . And yet one wonders why anybody should choose to live on Vatersay or Sandray, still less on Mingulay. The raiders in Edinburgh doubtless find the barriers of the Calton Jail irksome enough, yet they return to islands often veritably imprisoned by the sea.

It was stated recently on behalf of Lady Cathcart that Vatersay, while it affords excellent grazing, is not suited to cultivation . . . the raiders admit that Vatersay crofts would be only an adjunct at the best, a complement to the fishing, which is the staple industry of the islanders.

Many of the newspapers and opposition politicians claimed that the raiders were led by 'others' using the case for their own ends. Lady Cathcart issued a statement in *The Scotsman* of 24 June hitting back at the 'organised campaign of misrepresentation by political agitators . . . the public are being misled and deceived.' She questioned the hardships claimed to have been suffered by the raiders, citing the case of one of them (elsewhere identified as

Duncan Campbell) who had had a croft in Barra for ten years prior to 1901, during which he had paid only one pound of the twenty he owed for those years. She said that being fishermen they could make their living if they applied themselves to it (like her tenants on the coast of Aberdeenshire, she meant). She scorned the 'spurious public sympathy' for the raiders encouraged by the Lord Advocate's 'poor things' gaffe the previous summer.

One of the 'agitators' was, according to *The Glasgow Herald* of 18 July, 'an energetic emissary of the Land Values and Free Industry Union, Mr Kinloch. He came to prospect, but remained to address a meeting in Castlebay. He assured the men of Castlebay that the land reformers of Glasgow would stand by them. The assurance was of course warmly cheered, but a subsequent observation by the speaker that "he certainly thought they should break the law rather than starve" obviously struck his shrewd auditors as not quite prudent advice. It was received in solemn silence.'

A writer in *The Scotsman* of 14 July seized the opportunity to ridicule Scottish Secretary Sinclair for applying double standards: having taken no action over the raiding of Vatersay, for which he was widely criticised, he issued warnings to the raiders of part of the farm of Eoligarry, Barra, to desist. With breathtaking hypocrisy he claimed that 'the consequences might be most serious for themselves and their families . . . a heavy criminal responsibility will rest upon them as wrongdoers.' Regarding Vatersay, the writer's view was that 'if Sinclair shrinks from the use of gunboats for the vindication of the law he must take over the entire responsibility for Vatersay . . . he can only do this by purchase.'

The sentences were a humiliation for the government, and Sinclair in particular, since they had refused to initiate any legal action. The publicity, and scathing attacks on Sinclair in the House of Commons, put pressure on him to renew negotiations with Lady Cathcart. She had actually withdrawn her offer to cooperate with the Scottish Office because of its refusal to accept responsibility for paying compensation to the farm tenant for giving up his recently renewed lease. Sinclair caved in on this point, provided – and this did not emerge until the following year – that Lady Cathcart order the release of the men. Sinclair also agreed to provide a water supply; essentially he agreed to conditions originally set out by Lady Cathcart in October of the previous year.[7]

On 18 July it was announced that an agreement had been reached on the creation of crofts on Vatersay, and Lady Cathcart requested the court to order the men's immediate release. This being two weeks early, *The Glasgow Herald* of 20 July reported:

The public were unaware of what was transpiring, and consequently a probable public demonstration was avoided. The men emerged from the prison gates headed by Councillor Leishman and Mr Shaw, and were directed to the Regent Hotel, Waterloo Place, where a meal was provided. The procession of the men in that blue garb effected by fishermen attracted some attention, and those in the vicinity were quick to divine that the raiders had been set at liberty. Although the hotel is only a few hundred yards from the prison gates the men eagerly lit their pipes . . . Later, when the men were established in more comfortable quarters than those they had left, a 'Herald' representative had a talk with the men. They are not men to whom phrases leap readily to the tongue, but at the same time can express themselves with clearness and to the point. They were deeply grateful for the interest and practical sympathy evinced towards them . . . The men later in the day visited the Exhibition at Saughton, where tea was provided.

They left for Oban by train the same afternoon, and the next day, Sunday, they attended Mass in the Pro-cathedral. On Monday the party left for Castlebay, Barra, on board the steamer the *Lapwing*, and at Castlebay, reported *The Oban Times* of 25 July, 'They were met by large crowds of the inhabitants who extended hearty and enthusiastic greetings on their return home. Flags and bunting and stirring pipe music gave the occasion a gala aspect. The general feeling is one of relief and thankfulness that the hope that the government and Lady Cathcart would come to terms has not been disappointed. It may be mentioned that the men's fares home were paid by Lady Cathcart.'

It may also be mentioned that even in Barra support for the raiders was not universal, as is shown by a letter, signed by 'Islesman', published in *The Oban Times* of 18 July:

As a crofter of Barra myself, I see their action wrong. 'The Oban Times' said the settlers were on good terms with Mr MacDonald, the tenant of Vatersay, but how could anybody be on good terms with a man whose land they have seized in an illegal manner, and taken from him? . . . Mr MacDonald is one of the best men that ever lived; he is kind and good in every way to the poor people of Barra.

The cottars who came from Mingalay had good crofts. They first thought Vatersay was better than Mingalay, and moved over to it. They do not pay rent, and do not want to pay. Some Barra men now want to take land at Eoligarry. They are waiting to see what the result in Vatersay will be. They have told Mr MacGillivray that they mean to take possession.

Crofters in Barra who in previous years had allowed cottars to grow potatoes on their crofts may not have been sympathetic to the raiders, but were glad to be quit of the extra burden on their crofts, which could barely support a single family.[8]

The trial of the raiders propelled the Vatersay case into the headlines, more so than other cases. The raiding of farms in Barra, for instance, got very little publicity and the names of the raiders have long been forgotten. The main reasons for Vatersay's high profile were that the whole island was involved, and because of that the raiders took up residence rather than staked a claim from nearby and then returned to their homes, which happened in the other cases. The government was criticised for its failure to take early action against the raiders, thereby allowing them to establish themselves on the island, but if it had taken action to evict them, it would have been criticised for that. Had it bought Vatersay earlier it would have been accused of giving in to lawlessness. It would have been criticised whatever it had done; it was, as the above writer said, 'in a bog'. The trial fuelled public debate about the need for land reform, but instead of helping the government in its reform proposals, attention was focused on its handling of the case. The sentences were thus a humiliation for the government. At the same time, because of their leniency, they were seen as a victory for lawlessness, and as a moral victory for the raiders.

The debate over the case also showed that it was not simply a matter of land-hungry cottars seizing land which the landowner had refused them. Politics and politicians were also involved. Had the government used its powers to take legal action against the raiders, and/or bought Vatersay from Lady Cathcart, the case would have developed differently. It highlighted the differences in policy between the Conservatives and Liberals. It is interesting to speculate how the Vatersay case might have developed had the Conservatives been in power.

7. Purchase and division, 1908–1909

By the time the raiders returned to Vatersay from prison in July 1908, there were 172 people in thirty-two huts on Vatersay. This was an addition of only one hut since February; in the meantime people had been busy at the fishing. In August a report listed thirty-three households – families, couples, or single men. There were twenty-one households at what became Vatersay Township, near the farm; three each at Caolas and Uidh, and four at Eorasdail. Two people had built huts at Gortein, near the site of the later school, where there was a sheep fank (enclosure for shearing and dipping sheep) and wool shed; one of them, Roderick Campbell, had opened a shop. There was one family – of MacLeans, from Mingulay – at Beannachan.

Of the thirty-three households, fifteen were from Barra, sixteen from Mingulay (all but one at Vatersay and Eorasdail), one from Pabbay, and one from Eriskay. Most people were living in wooden huts, but nine had built stone and thatch buildings. Three families from Mingulay were on Sandray in three stone and thatch houses, and two others were building houses there. Six families remained on Mingulay. Two Mingulay families were recorded in Glen, near Castlebay, in November.

Three long-term Vatersay families were still in residence: Ann Ferguson at Caolas; Alexander MacDonald, shepherd, also at Caolas, and Archibald McCuish, who had been farm grieve for seventeen years, but had 'changed sides', and had been paid off by his employer. All three families eventually applied for and got crofts in Vatersay. The farmer Donald MacDonald and various farm workers were still living in Vatersay House.[1]

Now that the battle for Vatersay had been won (or appeared to have been won), letters of application for crofts began to arrive at the offices of the Congested Districts Board in Edinburgh. These were written on behalf of the applicants by educated people such as priests and schoolteachers, in English. The Board had already held a meeting, in May (1908), for prospective applicants, and thirteen fishermen from Kentangaval, for instance, all wanted crofts at Caolas. This application procedure seems to have been abandoned, however, because the following April the Board announced the application process which it then followed through.[2]

The assumption, or hope, among the existing settlers was that they would be able to stay on the land they occupied, so the applications were from people who had not yet settled there.

Applicants from Mingulay who had crofts there had to justify why they wanted a croft on Vatersay, since the stated purpose of the Vatersay scheme was to relieve 'congestion' caused by the large number of cottars in Barra. John Sinclair, father of the raider of the same name, explained:

It is true that I already hold a croft at Mingulay . . . being now an old man with only my two daughters staying with me (and even these are not prepared under any circumstances to stay longer in Mingulay) I am quite unable to earn a living in Mingulay. Having no family nor facilities for manning a boat I cannot depend on getting provisions from the main island even if I could earn the wherewithal to buy them. Last spring I bought some provisions in Castlebay but it was some three weeks before I could get them to Mingulay. The result was that the perishable portion was entirely unfit for use, while my family was nearly starving.[3]

Angus MacNeil:

Some ten years hence I occupied a holding in Mingalay but I had to submit it to Lady Cathcart through the death of my wife, leaving me with a young family of eight children. The land was not sufficient to maintain me and I had to leave the place to look for work on the mainland. The family were taken to Castlebay into the keeping of my sisters. I applied to Lady Cathcart's factor for a site for a dwelling house at Castlebay. In this I failed and having married the second time I have lived in my wife's house a poor helpless cottar.[4]

Negotiations between the Scottish Office (on behalf of the Congested Districts Board) and Lady Cathcart's agents proceeded during the summer of 1908. However, when the fine detail of the arrangements was being thrashed out, it became clear that certain points had not been clarified in the July agreement. The most important of these was the 'unfortunate misunderstanding' over the compensation payable to Lady Cathcart to cover the difference between the annual rent she had received from the farmer, £330, and the much lower rent, (eventually fixed at £180), she would receive from crofting tenants. The Board would have had to pay most, if not all, of the annual rent from the crofters over to her. The estate had demanded that the government would guarantee the rent, in other words that it would make up for any non-payment of rent by tenants. By the end of October 1908 it became clear that Secretary for Scotland John Sinclair and the Scottish Office had got themselves into an impossible situation and would have to buy Vatersay after all. So, having for nearly two years remained adamant that the government would not buy the island, Sinclair was forced into a humiliating climb-down, and of course the opposition and the press made the most of it when it became public at the end of February 1909.[5] A writer in *The Scotsman* of 26 February commented, with reference to the rumoured purchase and previous events, 'It is difficult for those who have not personal knowledge of the facts to realise how utterly the law has been discredited by the course which the government have taken in regard to this island.'

Sinclair, who had by now become Lord Pentland, had privately conceded a year earlier that it might come to this, and he later described the Vatersay affair as 'a miserably small business and a sordid bit of work.' He was inexperienced in crofting affairs and had difficulty understanding Lady Cathcart's reluctance to create another crofting settlement on an island. His under-secretary, Reginald MacLeod, had to explain it to him in specially simplified language.[6]

It only remained to settle the purchase price. The estate asked £7,500 but Lord Pentland managed to get it down to £6,500, the only stage in the protracted negotiations over Vatersay when the government got its way. The final figure for Vatersay, Sandray and smaller islands, purchase of the tenant farmer's sheep stock, and the costs of establishing the crofting settlement was nearly double that. In a letter to the Scottish Office, published in *The Edinburgh Evening News* of 29 April 1909, Donald Shaw, the raiders' solicitor, wrote that his clients considered the price to be 'excessive and out of all proportion to the value of the farm. They fail to see how the land can be made to pay on such a basis. If the rents are to be fixed so low that they produce only an inadequate return upon the money spent, my clients feel that they are being compelled to accept a charity which they do not desire.'

This attitude could partly explain the statement in *The Scotsman* of 22 April that, 'There is not the slightest gratification expressed by the raiders at the purchase of Vatersay. Some of their leaders do not conceal their dissatisfaction and discontent.' This was quite a change from the previous July, after their release from prison, when they wrote to Sinclair: 'We are genuinely grateful to you for bringing about this settlement.' They were dissatisfied also because they had hardly been consulted about the proposed crofting settlement. They felt that they should be involved in decisions affecting them, but that was not the Board's way, any more than it was Lady Cathcart's; however, commissioners of the Crofters Commission had consulted them when they visited Vatersay in August 1908 to compile a report on its suitability for crofting.[7] The process of allotting crofts would cause even more dissatisfaction.

Conditions in Vatersay, meanwhile, had become, according to a writer in *The Scotsman* of 26 February 1909, 'so bad that a number of the squatters have left the island, despairing of the prospects which at one time seemed to them so attractive . . . they have been so hard pressed during the winter that they are determined to try their luck elsewhere . . . the only persons who have taken benefit from the agitation are well-to-do merchants and prosperous crofters on the main island of Barra. It was by these persons that the stock grazed by the raiders on Vatersay was provided . . . It is almost impossible to state how many people are now on Vatersay as there has been a constant movement during the winter. The raiders have shifted between Barra, Mingulay, and Vatersay.'

And a writer in the edition of 22 April reported:

There is no one in authority on Vatersay and the raiders are doing as they please, cultivating small patches of land here and there where it can be done with the least exertion. The disadvantages which were foretold as inseparable from the cutting up of the land by crofter tenants have already begun to make themselves manifest. The sand is driven all over the island, so that there will be the greatest difficulty in getting the grass to grow. Another difficulty is presenting itself to the squatters, for no seaware has come ashore for manure . . . The people are becoming intensely dissatisfied,

and the probability is that by the time the Congested
Districts Board takes action for the formation of a crofter
settlement there will be a general desire to leave the island.
It need hardly be added that the government committed a
great blunder in connection with Vatersay.

The Congested Districts Board and the Crofters Commission
had, in fact, begun to 'take action' for creating crofts and the
necessary infrastructure such as fences, water supply, jetties and
paths. The Board proposed fifty-eight or sixty crofts in the four
townships where people had already settled. All had been
settlements before the evictions of 1850 with the exception of
Eorasdail, which had been settled in the more distant past. There
would be about twenty crofts at the farm, known as Vatersay,
eight at Eorasdail, sixteen at Caolas, fourteen at Uidh. All the
crofts at Uidh, and most of those at Caolas, would be strips of
land running north to south across the peninsulas. Each township
would have some designated common land for the grazing of
cattle; in the case of Uidh, this was Creag Mhòr, the area bought
by the Board for growing potatoes in 1903. Caolas and Uidh
would share the hilly ground of northern Vatersay as common
grazing for sheep, while Vatersay and Eorasdail would share
Sandray as common grazing. Each crofter had a certain number
of shares in the common grazing, and an entitlement to a certain
number of sheep; this was known as the 'souming'. Caolas and
Eorasdail had areas designated for potato growing as the croft
land was not considered suitable for the purpose. Crofts not on
the shoreline would have a means of accessing the coast to bring
in seaweed for fertiliser.[8]

Divisions among the settlers were revealed when Duncan Campbell removed the Board's wooden pegs marking out twenty crofts at Vatersay Township, and marked out twenty-four instead, claiming that Mingulay settlers would prefer more but smaller (one acre) crofts on Vatersay to being compelled to return to Mingulay. This resulted in fourteen opponents signing a petition against the changes; sixteen were in favour.[9] The final number of crofts was twenty.

Houses were not expected to be built on the crofts themselves, as is often the case in crofting areas, but near water supplies. In the case of Vatersay Township, twenty huts had already been built between the farm and the bay. The township consisted of two parts: the part built around the west side of the former farm buildings (where the southernmost houses are now) was called Baile Uachdrach, quaintly referred to as 'Upperton' by the English-speaking Congested Districts Board; the part where the majority of the houses were built, lower down towards the bay, were called Baile-Iochdrach, or 'Netherton' to the Board. Today the township is referred to simply as Am Baile, 'The Village'. The Eorasdail houses were to be near the beach, the Uidh houses near the jetty and at Caraigrigh. The Caolas houses were to be on the north side of the head of Bàgh Chornaig, and at the west end on the machair, but in the event, they were built on the crofts near the shore of the sound.

Water was to be provided by building concrete tanks on water courses to store a constant supply even in the driest weather, and water would be piped by gravity to stand pipes, one per township. Storage tanks were also built on springs. Contrary to the estate's earlier predictions, there was plenty of water even when there were nearly 300 inhabitants, and this water supply served the island until 1974. There were also three tiny lochs which could be used for watering stock, one at Caolas, one on the Uidh peninsula and one south of the farm, Loch Peigi. When the commissioners of the Crofters Commission visited in August 1908 in order to compile a report, they wrote of Loch Peigi, 'boys were actively engaged conducting a regatta with model sailing boats on this pond and wading knee deep through it.' [10]

Fuel for cooking and heating was a problem, for there was no usable peat on Vatersay – it had all been worked out by previous inhabitants – so coal had to be bought at great expense. The commissioners visiting in 1908 reported that some of the settlers planned to cut peat on the island of Muldoanich the following year. During the Second World War when coal was scarce, peat from Muldoanich was used again.[11] Coal was delivered by puffer, a flat bottomed vessel which would be grounded on a beach at high tide and unloaded as the tide receded (plate 20).

On 7 April 1909 the Congested Districts Board issued notices inviting applications for crofts on Vatersay. The notice announced:

The Congested Districts Board, having purchased the farm of Vatersay, propose to form about 58 or 60 holdings on the main island of Vatersay, namely, at Eorisdale, Vatersay, Uidh, and Caolis. No holdings will be formed on Sandray, which must be used solely for Grazing. As the sheep are on the ground and cannot be disposed of until October, possession of the new holdings cannot be given until Martinmas 1909. Applications for the proposed holdings are invited from landless cottars or squatters. All intending settlers must make formal application on forms, which may be obtained from Mr James Smith, Schoolmaster, Castlebay, or Mr Alexander MacDonald, Shepherd, Caolis, Vatersay. The Congested Districts Board desire to make it clear that none of the squatters currently on the farm are to be held as having thereby acquired a preferable claim to holdings. No application will be entertained from anyone who, after this date, squats on or takes possession of any part of the farm without the written authority of the Board.[12]

The settlers were furious about the statement that the selection process would take no account of whether the applicant was already on the island, and this was to become a source of great resentment. Donald Shaw said, in the letter mentioned above:

My clients inform me that there are some hundreds of people on the mainland of Barra and its neighbourhood who will probably make applications. As my clients have been in possession of a number of these holdings for the past two years or more, and have built their houses upon them, they do not consider that after the sufferings they have undergone they ought to be called upon to take their chance of allotment with such an overwhelming number of newcomers. It is needless for the Board to invite applications from outsiders unless it is proposed to remove some or all of the present occupants, and to repeat the painful judicial proceedings which have already entailed so much hardship upon them. They instruct me to say that they

must not be held responsible for any breach of the law
which may result from an attempt by the Board to place
newcomers on these holdings.

In a letter to J. Swift-MacNeil, a sympathetic MP of Barra descent,
the scribe Neil MacPhee wrote on behalf of Duncan Campbell and
others to request his assistance to 'resist the hand of the tyrant' by
which he meant the Board's proposals for what the settlers maintained were seventy crofts of unequal quality. The people moved
the pegs to mark out fifty-six crofts, and sent the names of fifty-six
prospective tenants to Sheriff Kennedy of the Crofters Commission.
They claimed that the few good crofts would be given to rich
incomers, and that the Board's intention was to 'turn men against
each other, and to keep the rich rich and the poor poor . . . it is better
to die in prison in the cause of truth and justice than to live a hundred
years a slave either to the blindness or the wilful tyranny of the
Board . . . the Board have acted all along in Barra in the interest of
the landlord and the oppression of the poor.'[13]

The application form for crofts asked the following questions
of applicants: in which township he would like a croft; name,
address, age, and occupation of himself, and ages of his wife and
children; and his amount of capital in a) cash, b) stock, or c)
fishing boat, and fishing gear. The form also required the
applicant to give two referees 'as to my character and ability
to manage a holding.' The completed application forms have
unfortunately not been preserved; however, the attitude of a
Board official to the applicants survives in the form of comments
he wrote on a 'census' of settlers compiled the previous November, such as 'no good', 'no means', 'good man', 'hopeless,

goes on two sticks'. Another official wrote of the settlers around the farm, '. . . their circumstances do not point them to be desirable crofters.'[14]

Applications were due in on 1 May 1909, and eighty-two were submitted. A 'Holdings Committee' chose the successful candidates in the middle of May. Three lists were drawn up. The A-list was men of good character with experience and assets, thus confirming that the main criteria for selection were ability to manage a croft, and assets in capital, stock or fishing gear. This had been the case when the Board selected applicants for crofts at Northbay Farm in Barra in 1901, the Board saying that the applicants with assets would thus be eligible for loans for houses and stock. The B-list was weaker candidates; the C-list was six men from Mingulay who had crofts there. There were twenty-two applicants from Mingulay (including three of the Sandray raiders). An official wrote that the Mingulay men had a 'high reputation for industry and good character' and would make good settlers.[15]

There was uproar when the names of the successful applicants were made public, for many of the original raiders were not among them, while some non-resident applicants from Barra were successful.[16] Neil MacPhee fired off two letters to Lord Pentland, the Scottish Secretary who was also Chairman of the Congested Districts Board, on 19 June. The first letter, from ten unsuccessful applicants including Hector MacPhee, Michael Campbell and John Campbell who had been imprisoned, demanded an explanation of why they were rejected, and said, 'We have been in possession for over two years and we are the lawful heirs of those evicted from this island sixty years ago . . . while others from the mainland of Barra are accepted to dispossess us. We know it, my

Lord, it is the Board's dastardly attempt to compel us to go back to the barren island of Mingulay. It shall never never be, my Lord, it is better a thousand times to die here than go through the same hardships which were our lot on that island.'[17]

In the second letter Duncan Campbell and twenty-seven other successful applicants,

> respectfully beg that our fellow cottars who were rejected be immediately restored to their respective holdings, or we beg that we too may share the same fate, for we cannot be so cowardly as to accept favours, and see our fellow men treated in this manner . . . we urge the government to send a competent neutral judge to compare the rejected tenants to those selected by the Board from the mainland of Barra, and to compare our division of the island with that of the Board. We beg further to demand an explanation of why the Board sent some of us by sham ballot from one end of the island to the other, while they granted special holdings to others, which were not balloted. Lady Gordon Cathcart's policy of rejecting us all was honourable as compared to the Board's mean methods.[18]

The granting of 'special holdings' applied to three applicants: Ann Ferguson, who had lived at Caolas for many years and was given the land she occupied, number 1 Caolas; William Boyd, the raider who was imprisoned, who was living at Gortein but was not allowed to remain there and was allocated 1 Uidh; and Roderick Gillies who got 3 Uidh. Reasons for giving the latter two preferential treatment were not stated.

The 'sham ballot' referred to was held to allocate successful applicants to crofts within townships. It took place in the school in Castlebay on 16 June, and the Board asked James Smith, schoolmaster, and Father MacKenzie, priest of Craigston, to conduct it, presumably to give it local credibility. In his report on the ballot, the Board's Angus Mackintosh wrote:

Duncan Campbell went into the school and asked all who had sent in their applications through Mr Shaw [their solicitor] to go out with him but no one went and he retired, and Hector MacPhee, who was an unsuccessful applicant, and Neil MacPhee were very excited and demanded to know what we were to do with those rejected and if we were going to 'sweep them into the sea'.

For each township, the slips with the names of the selected applicants and those with the numbers of the holdings were folded by Mr Smith and Father MacKenzie, and put into separate vessels from which they were drawn one by one, simultaneously by Mr Smith's boy or girl, each township separately.

The complaint that some people were sent 'from one end of the island to the other' probably referred to the fact that the twenty-three applicants were balloted for the twenty crofts in Vatersay, and the unsuccessful three balloted with the five applicants for the eight crofts in Eorasdail, so a few may have had to move to Eorasdail from Vatersay. Eorasdail had the least number of applicants, being the most remote, although the land was good.[19]

Neil MacPhee was scathing about the ballot. In a letter to Swift-MacNeil, he wrote: 'To give a plausible effect to their ballot the Board made a dupe of one of the priests of the island, Father MacKenzie, who had no idea of the intentions of the Board and had no knowledge of the size and value of the different holdings. He did not even know who was accepted or rejected until the whole thing was past . . . It is a well known fact that the Board have throughout the Highlands, as well as in Barra, showed a hostile spirit towards land law reform.'[20]

The rents for the crofts were also announced at the ballot. They were set as follows: Vatersay and Eorasdail, which had the best crofts, £3.10s; Caolas, which was intended mainly for fishermen, £2 17s; Uidh £2 12s. This gave a total rent for Vatersay crofts of £180, only just over half its rental value as a farm, but the Board also hoped to let Vatersay House. Board officials had considered setting the rents higher, but feared that the best applicants would not accept the crofts. The Board proposed rewarding those applicants who had not raided Vatersay by not charging them rent for their first year, a somewhat self-defeating exercise which would have resulted in an even lower rental income.[21]

In August Neil MacPhee wrote on behalf of himself and fourteen others to the Lord Advocate for Scotland (now Alexander Ure, who had replaced Shaw of the 'poor things' gaffe):

Your Lordship has stated on the floor of the House of Commons that the Congested Districts Board do not propose to import any cottars to the island. This is not the case. The Board are preparing to import single penniless young men from Barra with neither stock nor experience of holdings, and at the same time are preparing for the removal from the island of persons, with large families, whose character is irreproachable, whose stock is already on the island, and whose skill and ability to work holdings leaves no room for doubt.

In view of the Board's intentions to remove the rejected cottars now on the island, we do not understand how this can be effected when we have it on your Lordship's authority that 'No government and no proprietor has a right to deport grown up men and women from one part of the country to another, unless as criminals.'

We have been informed by the Secretary for Scotland that 'the Congested Districts Board bought Vatersay not for the squatters on the island but to relieve congestion in Barra.' My lord, need we again repeat that it was 'to relieve congestion in Barra' that we took possession of a few acres each on Vatersay, and are we again to be punished for taking the initiative in a step which the government itself approved.

The reply from the office of His Lordship expressed the hope that 'you will acquiesce peaceably with Lord Pentland's decisions.' [22]

The Board was unmoved by protests, also by offers by unsuccessful applicants to pay rents in advance, or to take up crofts at a new crofting settlement at Eoligarry, Barra. On 4 September the Board wrote to the twenty-four rejected applicants asking them to confirm within ten days their willingness to cooperate, that is, to leave Vatersay. As if anticipating resistance to their eviction, the Board intended to keep five or six crofts which they thought would not be taken up by the people to whom they had been allotted, free for such resisters.[23]

By now Lord Pentland had completely lost his authority and was being repeatedly criticised, not least by *The Scotsman*, for instance on 20 May: 'Vatersay is as a millstone hung on the neck of the Secretary for Scotland. At last Lord Pentland realises that it is a "wretched business". Last night when catechised and severely condemned in the House of Lords he was as elusive as a piece of thistledown blown about by every current of air.' The condemnation was for his handling of Vatersay in general, and in particular for not including a certain letter in the official correspondence on the Vatersay affair. That letter had revealed that he had offered to negotiate with Lady Cathcart on the matter of compensation to the tenant of Vatersay in July 1908 provided she order the release of the raiders from prison, which she did. In the opinion of the *Scotsman* writer, the letter was 'the key to the right appreciation of all that subsequently happened . . . Lord Camperdown [who had exposed Pentland] has done public service in keeping the Vatersay question before Parliament. It has ceased to be a meagre affair affecting only a small island. Law and order in the Hebrides are involved.' The writer in *The Scotsman* concluded that the people of the Hebrides were 'being dangerously misled by the freaks of the Scottish Office.'

With reference to further land raids in Barra (Eoligarry), South Uist (Milton Farm), Skye (Scuddaburgh Farm, Kilmuir), and Lewis (Dalbeg), a writer in *The Scotsman* of 22 June asked:

Is it too late for Lord Pentland to put an end to land seizures
in the Hebrides? He must now be sensible of the deplorable
error into which he was led, partly by the illegal instinct of a
Lord Advocate and partly by his own lack of clear dis-
cernment. Crofters and cottars in every part of the Islands
and Highlands have watched the conflict in Vatersay; they
have watched how much they may dare to do; a fiery cross
of licence is passing from district to district. Presumably it
will be impossible for landlords to let a farm on the expiry
of a lease, for no tenant will care to face vexation and
tyranny like that of which the occupant of Vatersay has
been the victim . . . Lord Pentland is now in the tightest
grip of his Hebridean delinquencies.

The last jibe referred to the crisis now looming caused by twelve
unsuccessful applicants for Vatersay crofts who were refusing to
give up the land they occupied and, it seemed, were going to
have to be evicted by force. Neil MacPhee wrote, 'The people
on Vatersay will not readily submit to a repetition of the evictions
of fifty-eight years ago on this island.' [24]

In September 1909 the Board sent out tenancy agreements for
successful applicants to sign in order to take up their crofts
formally from Martinmas (11 November). Duncan Campbell
and Neil MacPhee, who both got crofts at Vatersay Township, at
first refused to sign because MacPhee maintained that details in
the agreement were contrary to the Crofters Act. Angus Mackintosh, the Board's land manager, in a letter to Lord Pentland,
wrote that MacPhee 'said he would never sign anything not in
the Crofters Act.' MacPhee and Campbell tried, unsuccessfully,

to stop other tenants signing, and MacPhee 'worked himself into a state of excitement when I told him he must let the others exercise their own judgement.' Sheriff Kennedy, chairman of the Holdings Committee, wrote, 'I am surprised at MacPhee, who is a man of good education but he and Duncan Campbell seem determined to give us as much trouble as they can. If a fight must come – it is their own doing.' In another document there is a reference to 'the Campbell–MacPhee camp' and they, together with Neil MacPhee (junior) and his brother Hector (who did not get crofts initially) are referred to as the 'ringleaders', presumably in stirring up dissent. Duncan Campbell and Neil MacPhee (senior) did sign in November, after being threatened with losing their crofts.[25]

Neil MacPhee criticised the Board for sending Angus Mackintosh to get people to sign the tenancy agreements rather than going through their solicitor, Donald Shaw. Mackintosh had given the impression that if they did not sign, they would lose their crofts. MacPhee said that Shaw might have advised against signing, because the agreements were not entirely in accordance with the Crofters Act as was claimed.[26]

Mackintosh, in the above letter, raised a fair point about the selection criteria, as well as expressing personal views. He said that 'MacPhee and his cousins had a big stock in Mingulay and fenced off a large portion of the island for their own use. They have a considerable stock of sheep there still . . . their boat earned £500 this year . . . a splendid fishing season. They should be sent back to Mingulay. They have no sympathy among the general body of settlers.' The case of the Mingulay people who had crofts in Mingulay and were comparatively well off *was* different from that of some of the Barra cottars who had nothing, and if there was resentment against Mingulay crofters who got crofts in Vatersay among Barra cottars who did not, it would not be surprising. There was some coolness towards John MacLean from Mingulay when he took up his croft at Caolas, for he had three cows while many of the other tenants, most of whom came from Kentangaval, had none; and he was not given his share of the potato ground on the machair.[27]

The Sandray raiders, meanwhile, all of whom were from Mingulay, wrote a letter of application for crofts there in October 1908. Of the six men who had raided Sheader nearly a year earlier, three were still there in July 1908: John Gillies, John MacNeil and Donald MacNeil. Some elder sons were with them at that time, and the rest of their families had joined them by October. By this time two of the original raiders, who had gone back to Mingulay, had returned to Sandray with relatives, and were building houses: John MacKinnon with his brother, Alexander, and Michael MacNeil, and his aunt Flora MacNeil. A month later twenty-seven people in five houses were recorded, and the ruins of five houses, partially joined together in an irregular 'terrace' facing the beautiful sheltered beach, can be seen at Sheader. The houses were basic: they had fireplaces and chimneys, but no windows in the walls; these were at the base of the thatch. The westernmost house was Donald MacNeil's, the next probably John MacNeil's. This house was excavated by archaeologists in 1995 (see p. 36). The floor was found to be unpaved, apart from stone paving around the fireplace in the western wall, and there were signs of a partition separating the eastern end of the house from the remainder. The middle house is incomplete, some of its stones having been used to build or modify its eastern neighbour, the largest house. This was probably occupied by John Gillies, who stayed longer than the others.

In their application, the raiders said, 'We are satisfied that it is a most suitable place for us as lobster fishing to make a fairly decent living and we will be very thankful if we are given holdings here instead of the impossible place of Mingulay where hitherto we have been trying to make a living among such dangerous surroundings.'[28]

The Sandray raiders were not allowed to stay. The Board considered that there was not enough good arable land to support a viable crofting population, and even if there had been, such a community would have needed facilities and services such as education which would be expensive. Nor did the crofters of southern Vatersay want them to stay. It was reported in *The Scotsman* of 14 July 1908 that the raid had 'incensed the Vatersay squatters who had designed to occupy the island and who resent the intrusion of the Mingulay people.' In any case, the townships of Vatersay and Eorasdail were to have Sandray as common grazing for their sheep. The Congested Districts Board told the raiders to leave in April 1909, when it had bought Sandray along with Vatersay, but some of them stayed until they got crofts on Vatersay, and others returned to Mingulay. John Gillies and his family, the last inhabitants of Sandray, remained until they moved to Caolas in March 1911.[29]

Dom Odo Blundell described a visit to the Sandray community in October 1909, accompanying Father Hugh Cameron, the Castlebay priest, on a sick call.

The cottage, where lived the old lady who was ill, was most scrupulously clean, and she herself had that air of dignity and refinement which one so often meets in the Highlands. As a child she had lived in Sandray, but her parents had been evicted, and throughout her life she had longed to return. She had no family. A niece of hers married and went to Sandray with her. A short time previously her nephew, without asking leave of laird, factor, or anyone else, had sailed across from Barra [Mingulay, in fact] with his few sheep and other effects and had settled on the old family croft. He rebuilt the house, sowed his plot of potatoes, and was joined by two other cousins and their families. The children were the nearest approach to angels in human form that Father Cameron or I had ever seen. There were four of them, the only children on the island, and the happiness and joy of life which shone in their faces was a real pleasure to behold.

This account was clearly written long after the event and is not entirely accurate. If the old lady was in fact the mother rather than the aunt of the people mentioned then the account fits the known facts: she was Ann MacNeil, who was born on Sandray and moved to Mingulay following the eviction of the entire population in about 1835. In 1909 she was living at Sheader with her daughter Flora Gillies and son John MacNeil, who had all come from Mingulay. She died on Sandray the following April, and, as there was no burial ground in use there, her body was taken to Mingulay for burial, the last islander to be interred in the graveyard there. Alternatively the old lady could have been Flora

MacNeil, who was living at Sheader with her nephew Michael MacNeil, one of the original raiders, although she was born on Mingulay.[30]

By the end of 1909, therefore, the jubilation over the agreement reached between Lady Cathcart and the government in the summer of 1908 to create a crofting settlement on Vatersay had turned sour over the acrimonious process of applying for and allocating crofts. Legal action had to be taken to evict some of those whose applications failed. The process also revealed divisions among the settlers: Duncan Campbell and Neil MacPhee were not always supported in their attempts to influence others.

Scottish Secretary Lord Pentland continued to be criticised and ridiculed for his handling of Vatersay. The criticisms were, specifically, for the inadvertent encouragement which that handling had given to raiders in other places; for his being forced to buy the island having maintained for two years that he would not; for trying to cover up the events leading to the release of the raiders from prison and renewal of negotiations with Lady Cathcart in July 1908. In the press reports before and during the trial he comes across as well-intentioned but weak, even naïve. A year later, having had to perform gymnastics in order to get out of the many holes he had dug for himself, he seems somewhat beleaguered and hapless. He had become isolated in his own government since the death of his main ally, Prime Minister Campbell-Bannerman, in 1908.

8. Establishing the community, 1910–1913

By the beginning of 1910, ten of the unsuccessful applicants for crofts in Vatersay were holding out against eviction from the houses and land they occupied. Hector MacKinnon of Caolas found himself being assisted in his efforts to stay in an unexpected way. Mrs Margaret Burnley Campbell of Ormidale, Colintrave, Argyll, who had employed him in the past, somehow found out that he had been rejected, and wrote to the Congested Districts Board asking why. She said that she had never known a 'more hard working and honest fellow.' The Board's reply was that he had no capital, stock or boat, or share in a boat, which was a drawback since he was applying for a croft in the fishing township of Caolas, but they might be able to offer him a croft in a new scheme in Kilmuir, Skye! There was no recognition on the writer's part that it might be unlikely that a Barra family would voluntarily move to distant, Protestant, Skye. This shows how out of touch Board officials were. In MacKinnon's case it would have been ironic if it had happened, since his ancestors had come from there in the late eighteenth century as ground officers (factors) for the MacNeils of Barra.

Hector MacKinnon had been a cottar in Kentangaval, Barra, living 'in a kind of a house at the edge of the shore on a rock' with his wife Mary (MacPhee), from Mingulay, and six children, the youngest being Nan, who became celebrated as the bearer of Mingulay folklore and song. In evidence given to the Holdings Committee, he was quoted as saying, 'I worked here and there where I could get employment as a labourer or otherwise.' He was among the raiders of Vatersay of 28 July 1906, and had subsequently built a stone and thatch house at Caolas. The family was in residence by August 1908.[1] Nan MacKinnon described the house many years later to Barbara MacDermitt, who wrote the following account: 'Bent (marram), which grew along the shore, was used for the thatching and placed over a layer of peaty turf to seal the roof. The walls were thick stone. There were several windows and two chimneys, one at each end. Inside, sand was spread on the earthen floor in place of carpet, fresh white sand brought from the island beaches. The house was divided into three or four rooms according to need. Everyone slept in big box beds with a roof over them. Thick curtains hung at the front making them warm and sheltered.'[2]

When crofts were laid out in 1909 the land became 2 Caolas, and MacKinnon had hoped to be able to stay there, but the croft was allotted to John MacLean (Barnaidh) from Mingulay in May 1909. By this time another house had been built there, by John MacSween who died shortly afterwards leaving 'Widow MacSween', as she was referred to by the Board.

Mrs Burnley Campbell wrote to the Board again asking how much capital, which she would raise on his behalf, would secure

MacKinnon a croft; the reply was, about £15. Although the Board had initiated legal proceedings to evict him and others in September 1909, an official wrote to Mrs Burnley Campbell in December saying that they would not enforce eviction until the following spring, to allow her time to raise the capital, £20 or £25 now being mentioned. In April 1910 the Board wrote to her to say that MacKinnon 'persists in cultivating part of land in Vatersay let to others', and asking her if she could influence him to desist so that the Board would not have to enforce eviction. A month later one Board official wrote to another: 'The Board did not decide to give him one of the holdings which have already been renounced. Meantime Mrs Burnley Campbell might be able to persuade Hector not to be taking violent possession of land belonging to other people so as to make it easy for the Board to give him a vacant holding should a vacancy occur . . . Mrs Burnley Campbell should be told whether Hector will get the first chance of a vacant holding. It is hardly fair that she should be encouraged to take all the trouble in collecting subscriptions unless she is to have some assurance that he is to get a croft.'[3]

At the same time MacKinnon came under further pressure to move when John MacLean wanted to move in. He had already moved to Vatersay from Mingulay and had been living in Roderick Gillies's old house at 3 Uidh (the house was too near a well, and sanitary regulations obliged him to build another house further away), but Gillies wanted MacLean to move out. In August 1910 the Board offered MacKinnon 7 Uidh which had been renounced by its original tenant. In September, John MacLean put up a wooden hut on 2 Caolas, the fourth dwelling on it, prompting a Board official to write that it 'looked like a village' (Mary Mac-

Kinnon's sisters were also living there). In December an official wrote that MacKinnon was unsure whether to take up 7 Uidh or return to Barra, and that 'Hector says he has had every injustice from the Board . . . he and his wife rather think they were badly treated by the Board in not getting 2 Caolas.' It is not surprising that they felt aggrieved, but considering that their benefactress Mrs Burnley Campbell stepped in after the allocation of crofts had been decided, the Board could hardly have acted otherwise. The Board were very tolerant of his delays – no doubt influenced by Mrs Burnley Campbell – which were very inconvenient to John MacLean and his family. According to family tradition Mrs Burnley Campbell gave MacKinnon a boat (perhaps with the money raised) which he used to get to the fish factory at Orosaigh, Castlebay, where he worked.[4]

The saga dragged on. In May 1911 MacKinnon had still not moved from 2 Caolas, so he was served with an eviction order. A month later he was said to be living in a shed at Caolas and to be building a house at Caraigrigh, Uidh, which he finally moved into in August. At the same time Widow MacSween's wooden house was demolished, and MacKinnon's old house was unroofed.[5]

Many years later, Nan MacKinnon, Hector's daughter, talked about some of her memories of life at Caolas and Caraigrigh:

Your first task in the routine of the day, you had to put a good fire on, get your dough and start your baking. And you had to bake enough to do till the next day. There were no loaves coming to the island of Barra . . . You know there were no ploughs in our place. So it all had to be dug with a spade. So all hands were on deck. Everyone was included except the one that was kept in to do the baking. You had to have dinner ready, which of course was a pot of potatoes and fish. As often as not you could get mackerel, and herring was very plentiful at the time . . . and that's the way we lived.[6]

Meanwhile, other rejected applicants, including some of those, like MacKinnon, who faced eviction, eventually got crofts which their original tenants had not cultivated or built houses on. Eviction proceedings against them were therefore dropped. In March 1910 there were seven such crofts and some of these were given to Mingulay people, including raider Hector MacPhee, described the year before as one of the 'ringleaders' in causing trouble for the Board. Other unsuccessful applicants continued to live with relatives who got crofts, such as Michael Campbell (Teic) from Mingulay who lived with his nephew, Duncan Sinclair, and was said not to be aggrieved that his application for a croft was unsuccessful. Others left Vatersay altogether. Some successful applicants were also causing difficulties for the Board. In early 1910 Roderick Campbell at Gortein refused to take up a croft he had been allocated at Eorasdail, although he finally did so at the end of 1911. He had to be evicted from Gortein and the Board seized and sold off his possessions to recover the legal costs. He was suspected of shebeening – selling alcohol – from his shop. William Boyd also at Gortein had understood that he could have a croft there (a Board official commented that his knowledge of English was very limited), but he had been allocated 1 Uidh. He later took on 2 Uidh instead.[7]

By April 1910 all fifty-eight crofts had been allocated, but there were further changes over the next two years as some people decided not to take up their crofts, and these were used to accommodate applicants who had been unsuccessful previously, and most of the remaining people on Pabbay, Mingulay and Berneray.[8]

Donald MacDonald, the farmer, left at Martinmas (11 November) 1909 and a Board official compiled a report on Vatersay House and the farm buildings. The house comprised hall, parlour and dining room on the ground floor, five bedrooms on the first floor, and three rooms for servants in the attic. There were two single-storey extensions at the back: one comprising kitchen and dairy; the other (later demolished), the old schoolroom, which was by now roofless, the old kitchen, and an earth closet. The building was in generally good condition although some slates were missing at the front of the roof and rain was getting in and spoiling ceilings. General dampness was causing wallpaper to peel off walls. The Board intended to let the house eventually, and estimated £50 would need to be spent on it, but in the immediate term it was likely to be used as a temporary school and teachers' accommodation.[9]

The Board declined a request from Donald MacNeil, Sandray, to use the kitchen as a temporary home while he was building his house in Vatersay Township, but it did allow the ground floor rooms of the house to be used for two wedding parties, free of charge. In January 1910 Mary Sinclair, originally from Mingulay, married Roderick MacLean from Glen, and the following month Donald MacDonald married Catherine MacPhee, both originally from Mingulay. Both grooms signed undertakings to be responsible for any damage to the house, but none occurred; they were asked to 'wash out the house afterwards.' A Board official reported Duncan Campbell as saying that the Board 'were not to give the house to anyone as it is to be kept for dances, concerts and weddings.' The official commented, 'Evidently there's a good time coming!'

On another occasion, in January 1912, Neil MacPhee reported on a wedding party at the house: 'Although the key could not be found everything was carried out satisfactorily. Admittance was gained by a window on the second floor which was not fastened inside. Three rooms were used, the principal room for dancing, the parlour for the table and the kitchen for cooking. Only three persons in the whole gathering tasted strong drink.'[10]

Of the other buildings belonging to the farm, the former steading below Vatersay House had been taken over by the settlers. The buildings on the west side were already ruined in 1906 when the raiders attempted to rebuild walls for temporary dwellings. Of these, the official reported 'nothing now remains except the ruins . . . on the site of these buildings four hovels have been formed' and were occupied by single elderly people. The southernmost houses of Vatersay Township now occupy this area. The buildings on the east side of the square, built of stone with turf roofs, were being used as byres. The grieve's house, a small stone and thatch house, was still occupied by McCuish who had got a croft at Vatersay Township. The shepherd's house at Caolas, a large stone and thatch house on what had become 5 Caolas, was still inhabited by the MacDonalds, who had also got a croft at Vatersay Township, and would be moving there. The only other buildings from the farm era were the corrugated iron wool shed and dipper shed at Gortein, to the west of the site where the 1927 school was built.[11]

Apart from the few stone and thatch houses, most of the settlers still lived in wooden huts with felt roofs. The Mingulay people, who had lived in traditional houses with thick stone walls and thatched roofs, must have disliked these flimsy 'boxes'. Later, more permanent houses were built of wood or of corrugated iron on wooden frames, lined internally with matchboard. These houses had stone fireplaces at one end, and three of these freestanding fireplaces can be seen at the now-deserted township of Eorasdail where they are all that remain of the wooden houses they once served. Two other ruins at Eorisdail are of another common type of house, which had stone gable walls incorporating fireplaces and chimneys, and corrugated iron side walls. One house of this type survives intact in the township of Vatersay. It was built in 1932 by Johnathan MacLeod, and was last inhabited by his sister-in-law, Nan MacKinnon, who died in 1982. In a third type, also represented at Eorasdail, all four walls were of stone. The Board did not stipulate house designs but they had to be approved by the engineer, Walter Coles, and houses had to be built within three years of taking up the croft. Duncan Campbell built his house walls entirely of stone, the first settler to do so, and this house is the only one to survive, still in use and largely unaltered, from this early building period. He was given permission in 1910 to quarry stone from the high ground of 7 and 8 Vatersay (he had 6), north of Vatersay House, and had begun to build by August 1911 when he asked the Board for scaffolding. The house was unique at the time in having two full storeys with storm windows, as befitted the leader of the community. Coles wrote, 'It will be quite a superior house when completed.' The house is on the right hand side of the road, and the first of three houses, as you enter the township. [12]

Tenants could get loans of up to £12, repayable over fifty years, towards building their houses, but in February 1912 Neil MacPhee – who had by now become the Board's ground officer or factor – wrote to the Board on behalf of many of the tenants saying that this was not enough, and requesting £50 grants for building stone houses which would remain the property of the Board. MacPhee suggested that 'a house on every second holding in Caolas and Uidh would be enough as it is possible that some may wish to remove to other districts under the new Land Act, holdings as they stand being too small.' The act was the Small Landholders (Scotland) Act of 1911, which the Liberal government finally pushed through after failed attempts in 1906, 1907 and 1908, and MacPhee was anticipating people applying to enlarge their crofts or moving to larger holdings elsewhere. A Board official wrote at the time: 'If some tenants want to flit we must be very cautious about making loans,' adding, 'Some of the Vatersay huts are hardly fit for human habitation.' Another official used the word 'shanties'. [13]

James Cameron wrote in 1910, 'The township of Vatersay looks like some Canadian lumber camp. The wooden sheds erected for dwellings are of the most primitive kind. In some instances the sheds have to be fastened with wire ropes to the earth or the bare rock. Without these fixtures the first gale would blow them down.' Neil MacPhee praised the people of the township in 1912: 'Their cooperation in equipping the township with horses and carts and other implements would do credit to people with more capital.' They had brought a coal steamer direct from Glasgow saving nine shillings per ton on the price at Castlebay.[14]

MacPhee's remarks about the small size of the crofts were echoed by Cameron in 1910: 'The serious defect of the Vatersay settlement is the size of the holdings.' He also drew attention to the lack of peat and the high cost of coal. These were the two main criticisms of the Vatersay settlement. Others were the sandy soil in places and the problem of sand drift.

Many people also built byres for their cattle in the traditional way – stone with thatched roofs. People from Vatersay and Eorasdail townships got the bent (marram) for thatching from Sandray, even though they had agreed not to do this as the roots stabilise the sand and prevent it drifting. The ruins of byres at Eorasdail and elsewhere can still be seen.[15]

There were many other aspects of the new crofting settlement to be sorted out. In the autumn of 1910 the Congested Districts Board built a path from the head of Bàgh Chornaig along its southern shore to meet the existing track which ran from the pier at Uidh towards the farm. This path (the road now follows the route) was primarily for the use of Caolas children attending the school at Gortein. There was a central route along the Uidh peninsula but it was not made up into a path until later. Eorasdail never got a path, apart from a short stretch at the township end, as most of the route to Vatersay Township was fairly easy and dry. Three concrete jetties were built in 1912: one at Uidh, which remained the main landing place for the island until 1979, another at Caolas, and the third at the southern corner of Bàgh Bhatarsaigh. Eorasdail did not get one, there being no sheltered location. The water supplies for each township had been completed in 1909.[16]

The machair, the sandy areas bordering beaches at Caolas, Uidh and the isthmus joining the two parts of Vatersay, was not to be cultivated because there was severe wind erosion of the sand if the turf was stripped off, as had already happened. The problem of sand drift and the need to contain it was mentioned as early as 1845, when it was worsened by rabbit burrows. It is still a concern today and old fishing nets are being used to stabilise sand where it is being eroded. The crofters of Vatersay Township decided to repair wind damage to the machair every November. Some people stored potatoes in clamps in the machair.[17]

There was a dispute among the crofters of Uidh in 1912 when one of them reported several others to the Board for planting potatoes at Uidh Gheal (the west side of Creag Mhòr, around the beaches), which was meant to be reserved for cattle grazing. The crofters said their crofts were 'very poor and not a success' and they needed potato ground like the other townships had. Eventually there was agreement that the ground could be used for potatoes. However, it was not very productive, being part of the area bought by the Congested Districts Board for growing potatoes in 1903 and found to be useless.[18]

It was reported in 1910 that there was some interest in using Mingulay for grazing, but the Board and Lady Cathcart were opposed to this. Neil MacPhee, who had a large number of sheep, attempted unsuccessfully to rent crofts in Berneray after it was abandoned, and also in Mingulay, to use for grazing. The following year some tenants from Barra who had not yet taken up their crofts in Vatersay were said to be subletting their share of

the common grazing to Barra merchants, and using the income
to buy provisions at the merchants' shops. The subletting was
contrary to the terms of the tenancy agreements and the un-
tended stock was annoying to the residents. Some tenants got
into debt and then the merchants took their stock as payment.[19]

In April 1911 the Congested Districts Board heard of a
'rumour that Lady Cathcart had let, as from Whitsunday, the
Islands of Pabbay, Berneray, and Mingulay to one grazing tenant,
and that notice has been served on the people resident on those
islands that they are to leave, and that their stock if not cleared off
will be seized.' Until then there had been no policy of resettling
the inhabitants of those islands, which still belonged to Lady
Cathcart, on Vatersay. Leaving was at first a matter of individual
choice, but once some people left, it became clear to others that
life would become difficult if not impossible. Some people did
not want to leave, but knew they had to. John MacLean of
Mingulay for instance was doing well at fishing. Four or five men
were needed to man a boat, and the populations of Pabbay and
Berneray, which had only three families each before 1907, were
only just viable. In the case of Mingulay, only six families
remained in August 1908 and, although some people returned
for varying periods, the population dropped further in 1910
when the school closed. By 1909, twenty-two Mingulay families
or individuals (including those on Sandray) had applied for crofts
on Vatersay, and eight of these had been unsuccessful, but nearly
all of them got crofts there eventually. By April 1911 eleven
adults remained on Mingulay, none of whom had applied for
crofts on Vatersay in 1909. They included the MacKinnon
brothers and Michael MacNeil, all three of whom had been

living on Sandray in 1908, and John MacKinnon and Michael MacNeil were photographed on Vatersay in August 1909 (see front cover). These last inhabitants were elderly or unmarried or both, and some of them were reluctant to leave. Six people in two families remained on Pabbay, and none on Berneray; Peter Sinclair, the last inhabitant, had been unsuccessful in his application for a croft on Vatersay in 1909, and he left sometime after a further attempt failed in late 1910.

The grazing tenant was Jonathan MacLean of Barra, also a merchant and hotel-keeper, who had been taking over crofts on the islands as their tenants left. The Board was keen to avoid the remaining population squatting on Vatersay, so it found crofts there for those people who had nowhere else to go. Mary Campbell did not want to leave Mingulay and was one of the last to go. She did not get a croft, but lived in a traditional-style house at Beannachan, which was part of the common grazing of Uidh Township. The Board's 'policy of fetching the Mingulay islanders nearer civilisation' was completed in the summer of 1912 when the last inhabitant, Michael MacNeil (an Righ) moved to Eorasdail, Vatersay. The last year when fishermen were recorded on Mingulay was 1912; presumably they were former islanders who had moved to Vatersay but who based themselves there during the fishing season. It was a little ironic that these Mingulay men should return to the island they had been so keen to leave as a place of permanent habitation, partly on account of its drawbacks for fishing. Subsequently, Jonathan MacLean unroofed the houses and dismantled the derrick to prevent reoccupation. Pabbay had been abandoned by this time.[20]

The last of the Sandray raiders, John Gillies, had remained

there despite an order to leave in April 1909, and the Board began legal action to evict him later in the year. He had nowhere to go, as he had been unsuccessful in his application for a croft in Vatersay in 1909, unlike John MacNeil and Donald MacNeil. In the summer of 1910, by which time the Gillies family were the only people left there, the grazings committee of Vatersay and Eorasdail townships, which had Sandray as their common grazing, also tried to get him to leave. He was using the southern part of Sandray as grazing for his own cattle, but the committee wanted the whole island for their sheep; they had bought the stock already on the island. They allowed him to stay until Martinmas, but he still had nowhere to go until he was given 15 Caolas in December 1910. It had not been taken up by its original tenant. The materials for his house which he ordered from Glasgow arrived in February 1911. The house was the stone and corrugated iron variety, and the story is told that during the building, one of the stone gable walls fell down three times, so the priest was summoned to bless the stones and at the fourth attempt it stayed up! The family finally moved at the end of March 1911, and the children started school on the 27th, after a gap of about three years. Thus ended a long journey: John Gillies had first raided Sandray in November 1907, and his family joined him there later; they wanted to stay but were not allowed to and eventually were given a croft at Caolas.[21]

Moving to Vatersay must have been strange for the Mingulay people, and perhaps traumatic for some. Although most of them moved there, the relocation spelled the end of the close knit community, as they were scattered among four townships. There was no longer a need for many of their traditional communal activities such as hauling in boats, cutting peat, holding prayer meetings on their own, and waulking (fulling) the cloth they made. Because of their former isolation, the Mingulay people did not find it easy to fit in with the settlers from Barra. Mary Campbell always preferred Mingulay to Vatersay: it was wild in the winter but people were friendlier and more content, and they changed a lot when they moved to Vatersay. The harsh feelings some of the Mingulay people had about their island mellowed with time, and for many years they and their descendants went on annual pilgrimages to their former home. Neil MacPhee wrote an emotional song about it.[22]

The subject of education of the children of Vatersay had been raised many times since 1906. In January 1908 Duncan Campbell wrote to Barra School Board with a petition for a school from the parents of twenty-four children. The Board dismissed the appeal saying the petitioners had no right to be there. By November of the same year there were fifty-five children of school age, and the School Board said it would have to wait and see how the situation resolved itself. A writer in *The Scotsman* of 29 October 1909 criticised the 'scandalous neglect of children's education' and condemned the Congested Districts Board for demanding £10 per acre rent for the site for a new school, when Lady Gordon Cathcart had asked only 10s 6d (52.5p) per acre for the same purpose in Barra. A new building was needed because the two ground floor rooms of Vatersay House were too small, and it was too far from Caolas; regulations stated that children should not walk more than three miles to school. Gortein was chosen as the most central place.[23]

School opened in Vatersay House on 28 June 1910 with forty

pupils. Joseph Campbell from Barra was headmaster, a post he held for the next forty-one years. Sarah MacShane, the former teacher at Mingulay School, was assistant teacher. Mr Campbell recorded in the log book: 'Light and ventilation in the two schoolrooms are very poor making the work for both teachers and scholars very disagreeable . . . more than 75% of the children present have been away from school for the past three years with the result that they have forgotten almost everything that they have learned . . . I find the children very backward but I can see that they are very willing to learn.'

There were only thirty-four desks, these having come from Mingulay School which closed two months earlier. There were few slates or exercise books, so most work was oral at first. More desks and materials, including a wall-map of the British Empire, arrived in September. There was no heating of any kind until the first week of January 1911.

The site chosen for the new school was above the building of 1927 which still stands next to the road. The area is known as Cean Magaig locally. The new school was built cheaply, of corrugated iron, by Messrs Cowieson and Co., Glasgow, and had two classrooms. Houses for the head teacher and assistant teacher were built at a later date. Building began in the autumn of 1910, and workmen lodged with Roderick Campbell, who lived nearby. A 'shelter' for the children to use during breaks was built below, on a site now occupied by a chalet above the 1927 school building. The new school opened on 13 January 1911, with fifty-five pupils enrolled. Numbers rose steadily as more families moved into their crofts, until a peak of seventy was reached in July 1911, and the highest number recorded was seventy-two in 1913.

Education was entirely in English, although Gaelic was taught as a subject. Apart from the usual school subjects, there were classes in singing and physical education. The 1914 annual report stated, 'It is suggested that Managers might consider the proposal to introduce cookery to this school as a subject of practical instruction not only for senior girls but also for boys. Most of the latter, on leaving school, take up work on fishing boats where even a slight knowledge of cookery would be of benefit.'

The proposal was considered, and classes began in December. Evening classes for adults, known as 'continuation classes' were also held in the school, taught by the teachers. Subjects included those taught to the children but there were more practical classes too, dairying and navigation being mentioned.

Most of the early entries in the log book, which head teachers were required to keep, are about attendance. The children had to walk in all weathers with no proper waterproofs, so in very wet weather many did not set out. Sometimes they did set out, and turned up soaked. On occasion their struggle was to no avail because so few children turned up that they were sent home again. Children living at Eorasdail did not even have a path to walk on, and the parents of three children living there withdrew them from school in the winter of 1914–15. Attendance also dropped when the children were needed to help out during busy times on the croft in the spring and summer. The school was occasionally closed for several weeks at a time when there were epidemics of smallpox, whooping cough and mumps.[24]

Occasionally Mr Campbell, who lived in Barra at first, was unable to cross to Vatersay because of stormy conditions. Mrs MacShane, however, lived in Vatersay and tried to get a croft or at least a house. She was originally from Beauly, Inverness-shire, and had taught in Mingulay since 1904. She was a tough and formidable woman: when one of her children was born in Mingulay she didn't take a single day off work. As people started to leave in 1907, her husband, Edward, had taken over two crofts, and she applied on his behalf to the Congested Districts Board for a croft in Vatersay in advance of their move to the island in 1910. He was unsuccessful, and the family of seven appears to have lived in one room of Vatersay House for a time. Mrs MacShane asked the Board for permission to build a house next to the new school. The Board said this was a matter for Barra School Board, but an official expressed concern that there was a risk of the MacShanes squatting in Roderick Campbell's house when he moved to Eorasdail. When she demanded a categorical answer as to whether they would be allowed a house or croft anywhere in Vatersay the answer was no. A Board official wrote that she was 'a most difficult person to argue with or do business with and she means to have her own way.' Undaunted, she took her case to Lord Pentland, the Secretary for Scotland:

Your Lordship is quite aware how impossible – not to say indecent – for all of us to sleep in one room 12x12, for granted we are willing to put up with the 'Congestion'. My children all have been born on the soil and one of them died on it too, therefore they have a right to a home here . . . if the argument arises that the land is not for teachers you must remember that my husband is not a teacher but a landless cottar. The Board's decision is, my husband cannot get a croft because he is not a native of

Barra. But what of my children – are they not natives? What constitutes a native? My children born in Mingulay are surely natives. Their mother is teaching in Inverness-shire for nine consecutive years. Is she not naturalised yet? If the mainland was inhabited by no one but natives Scotland had need of immigration not emigration.

Needless to say, nothing came of the letter. Edward MacShane applied for permission to open a shop at Gortein after Roderick Campbell had gone, and this was approved subject to conditions. However, the family left Vatersay for Barrhead, Glasgow, in May 1912.[25]

The school employed a 'compulsory officer' whose job it was to chase up and, if necessary, report parents of children who did not attend regularly. In a small community where everybody knew each other and many were related, this must have been an invidious position. Offenders could be fined or taken to court in Lochmaddy, North Uist. On one occasion in the 1920s a mother who had been fined 5s for the non-attendance of her child came into school, grabbed a stick used as a pointer on the blackboard and hit Mr Campbell with it! There were frequent changes in the post holder, and Mr Campbell often recorded long periods when the officer did not turn up to collect the list of absentees. There was a similarly high turnover of cleaners. Edward MacShane held both posts in the early years. Once, when a cleaner, he was reported to have 'refused to do the monthly scrubbing.' Neil MacPhee (senior) was compulsory officer for a time.[26]

Vatersay House was returned to the Congested Districts Board in March 1911, and the Board attempted to let it. Advertisements in *The Scotsman* in April 1911 announced: 'To let, unfurnished, the farmhouse on the island of Vatersay, containing two public rooms, eight bedrooms, kitchen and other accommodation, with garden and a small plot of ground; the house is nicely situated in a sheltered position and commands a fine view.'

Naturally, the advertisements did not mention the less attractive aspects of the house, such as the 'fine view' including a good prospect of the motley collection of habitations of the new township of Vatersay, and the absence of any form of drainage or running water (this came from a well south of the house), although this was perhaps not unusual at the time. Replying to one enquirer on the subject of servants, Angus Mackintosh, the Congested Districts Board's land manager, revealed his attitude to the people of Barra and Vatersay by saying that, 'I am not sure that you could get suitable servants in Barra but you would have no difficulty in getting them from North or South Uist or Benbecula'.[27] The attempts to let the house seem to have been a complete failure.

The last element in the new island community to be provided was the Roman Catholic chapel in 1913. The raiders of July 1906 regarded Beannachan as a place of worship. Beannachan ('blessed place') is situated above the shore north of the school and according to tradition, Mass was held there in the seventeenth century, at a time when Catholic priests had to keep a low profile. Father Hugh Cameron (Maighstir Eoghan), parish priest of Castlebay, celebrated Mass there in 1906, and the raiders pledged that however illegal their seizure of the land had been it would be legalised in time. They also pledged that a church would be built.

Before 1913, Father Cameron came to Vatersay to attend a house Mass once a month, and on other Sundays the islanders would cross to Castlebay to attend Mass. The raiders' pledge was fulfilled in 1913 when the Church of Our Lady of the Waves and St John was built on part of 2 Uidh, offered by the tenant, William Boyd. The corrugated iron building was supplied by Spiers of Oban and was designed to accommodate 250 people. It is believed that it was funded by the Roman Catholic Marquess of Bute. The altar and benches were made by the Mingulay craftsman, John MacKinnon, now living in Eorasdail, and the altar rail came from St Columba's Chapel, Mingulay; it too had been made by him. The confessional door had been salvaged from the *Maple Branch* which was wrecked on Sgeir Lithinis off Sandray in 1897. A wing at the north end provided accommodation for the visiting Barra priest in case he was stormbound. The stone enclosure wall was built by the community. When the new chapel opened, Mass was held every Sunday at 10.30 a.m. by Father Cameron. There was also an evening service at 6 p.m. Confessions were heard on Saturdays.[28]

The raiding and settlement of Vatersay had taken eleven or twelve years, from the first raids to the completion of the initial allocation of crofts. This was a long time, by any standard, but Vatersay was only one of dozens of farms which were raided in the Hebrides and on the mainland during the period. Vatersay, however, got more publicity and caused more controversy than other raids. As James Cameron remarked in 1910, it was 'the theatre upon which was fought one of the keenest conflicts in the struggle for land reform in the Hebrides.' There were various reasons for this. The main distinguishing feature of the Vatersay case was that an entire island was involved, rather than a small part of an island or the mainland. This meant that the raiders effectively took physical possession and it would have been very difficult to dislodge them. The large number of people involved – up to about 170 – was also exceptional. The trial gave the case a lot more publicity. The long period between the first raids and the allotting of the crofts – three years in the case of some of the raiders – meant that many people had got established and there was a lot of bad feeling when some of them failed to get the land they had settled on and felt they had a right to.

Another factor was that the main period of raiding and the establishing of the crofting settlement, 1906–11, coincided exactly with the attempts of Scottish Secretary Sinclair to get the Small Landholders Bill through parliament, so the land issue was in the public eye. He was using Vatersay as a 'dry run' for the bill, but Vatersay did not work out as he would have wished. Every time there was a problem, and there were many, he was criticised and ridiculed in Parliament and in the press. His (mis-)handling of the affair merely encouraged raiders elsewhere; as *The Scotsman* of 23 November 1920 commented, 'The lesson was learned and forcible seizure has become a recognised method of acquiring land in the Long Island.' Raiding continued in crofting areas well into the 1920s, particularly by former soldiers having returned after the First World War, and only ceased when the demand for land was satisfied, and the steady decline in population meant that new holdings were not needed.

On a local level, the raids resulted in crofting tenants returning to Vatersay fifty-six years after their predecessors, in some cases their ancestors, were evicted. They also resulted in the three southernmost islands – Pabbay, Mingulay and Berneray – being abandoned by their inhabitants who settled in Vatersay.

9. Since the raiders

The new community flourished for many years. The population dropped only modestly, in line with the general trend in the Western Isles, from 288 in 1911 to 262 in 1921 and 240 in 1931. However, some of the criticisms of the crofting scheme which were made at the time it was taking shape cropped up again. A writer in *The Scotsman* of 23 November 1920 said, 'Vatersay was not suitable for small holders, being destitute of many of the requirements of a crofting community, and the settlement cannot be described as a success.' Alasdair Alpin MacGregor wrote in 1929 of 'two serious defects', the small size of many of the crofts and the lack of peat for fuel. But John Lorne Campbell wrote in 1936, 'Vatersay and Eoligarry are amongst the most successful settlements of the Board of Agriculture, whose standards of management have not been without influence elsewhere.'

Of the many Vatersay men who served in the merchant navy during the Great War five were killed. Some island women worked in the munitions factories in Glasgow. Bàgh Bhatarsaigh sheltered two ships which had been damaged during the war. The first was the ss *Aranda,* a Norwegian vessel carrying timber to Glasgow, which hit a stray mine off Skerryvore, near Tiree, in August 1916 and split in half. The stern half remained afloat on account of the timber and it was towed to Vatersay and dumped in the bay. The timber and hull were auctioned the following year but there were no takers for the hull which remained in the shallows of the bay until some time in the Second World War, when it was cut up for scrap. The second ship, the ss *Idomeneus,* owned by the Alfred Holt Line, was en route from New York to Liverpool when she was torpedoed by a German U-boat off the west of Ireland in September 1917. She was towed to Vatersay for repairs, and three 'Chinese' firemen who were killed in the engine room when the torpedo struck were buried in Vatersay. A memorial was erected in the Church of Scotland burial ground at Cuier, Barra, which states that they were buried at the *Annie Jane* monument and at 'Caragarie Point burial ground', meaning the graveyard of Cille Bhrianain on Uinessan. The body of a fourth crew member, who was from Cheshire, was returned there.[1]

The original corrugated iron school building of 1911 did not stand up well to the rigours of Vatersay's climate. The annual report for 1925 noted that it was neither wind nor water tight, and it was decided that a new building was needed. The following May (1926) the site for the new building, lower down the hillside, was chosen. Work did not start for a long time, however, and meanwhile the old building suffered flooding and damage during violent weather in January 1927. Some parents withheld their children as a result. The new building incorporated a teacher's house, and was built of rendered brick. The contractor was Campbell, Smart and Fraser. A toilet block was built at the rear, with its own water supply. It was formally opened on 22 November 1927. Pupil numbers had dropped considerably from the peak of seventy-two in 1913. There were thirty-five in 1925 and thirty-nine in 1928.[2]

MacGregor wrote in 1929 that 'a native of Vatersay who had travelled widely in his younger days deplored the fact that bricks had been used in its construction while thousands of tons of native stone were procurable at hand. And he described the erection as resembling the entrance to a factory built on the outskirts of a city.' MacGregor also wrote, 'at the present time the township of Vatersay is one of the tidiest in all the Outer Hebrides.'

The old school buildings were demolished in 1930. The concrete floors can still be seen on the hillside.[3]

The fishing industry based at Castlebay continued to provide employment for men and women during the season. The industry declined in the 1930s because of over-fishing of the herring stocks by trawlers based at mainland ports. Ironically, Michael Campbell (Teic), one of the raiders from Mingulay, worked on a trawler based at Fleetwood, Lancashire. This gave rise to the lower part of the township of Vatersay, where he lived, being referred to as Fleetwood, one of many examples of the islanders' great sense of humour.

The attempts of the Congested Districts Board, and its successor the Board of Agriculture for Scotland, to let Vatersay House came to nothing. Advertisements in *The Scotsman* in 1920 announced: 'Good situation and suitable for a gentleman's residence, or residence and shop combined.' It is recorded as vacant up to 1930, and in about 1935 the roof was taken off and some of the slates were used on a new house in Castlebay. The extension on the southern side of the back of the house, which was even longer than the surviving northern one, was probably demolished before the house was first advertised in 1911. In recent years there have been rumours that the ruin has been sold.[4]

The naturalist Seton Gordon wrote of Vatersay in 1935:

In certain respects the island of Vatersay is the most interesting of the Outer Hebrides. The people who live here are not natives in the true sense of the word, but migrated to the isle less than thirty years ago, some from Barra, some from Mingulay, a few from Pabbay. They are, even for Hebrideans, unusually friendly and unspoilt, hospitable and simple. The older people (from sixty years upwards) are unable to speak English, and their Gaelic is melodious and cultured. There is no peat on Vatersay and so (this is exceptional in a Hebridean island) coal is the only fuel. The houses on the isle are modern, and there are only two or three thatched houses. I believe that Vatersay, of all the Outer Hebrides, is the only island that is entirely Catholic . . . It was unexpected to hear that no weaver remained on the island, nor even a spinning wheel.

He went on to describe his meeting with a Vatersay man who had been brought up on Mingulay, and told him all about the methods of catching and cooking seabirds which had been used there. It is unlikely that there had been any working weavers among the settlers, since imported cloth and clothing were in common use early in the century, and the two remaining looms in Mingulay were left behind by their owners.

By Vatersay being 'in certain respects . . . the most interesting' of the Outer Hebrides, Gordon was referring to the survival of oral tradition and customs from a way of life which had practically died out elsewhere. Gordon wrote a few years later, 'I am sometimes asked in which island are still to be found the simple old-fashioned customs of the people. I think that on the island of Vatersay the old way of living is chiefly to be found at the present day.' The Mingulay people were the bearers of this tradition, and folklorists came to Vatersay to record songs and stories from them. John Lorne Campbell was the first to do so, in 1937. Recorders from the School of Scottish Studies in Edinburgh worked there from the 1950s up to 1981. One of them, Lisa Sinclair, who was from Vatersay, also recorded people talking about life on Mingulay and the raiding of Vatersay.[5]

Elizabeth Campbell (Ealasaid Chaimbeul) taught at Vatersay school from 1935 to 1937, and wrote about life at that time in her autobiography. She was from Bogach (Northbay) in Barra and lodged in Vatersay during the week. She found the people very friendly and courteous. They would gather in someone's house in the evenings for informal ceilidhs, where songs were sung and stories were told. Mingulay people would reminisce about their former home. At weekends she returned to Barra if the weather was favourable, and on Sunday afternoon began the journey back. She walked the six miles to the end of the road at Nask, over the boggy shoulder of Bentangaval and down to the shore opposite Caolas. One of the men of a Caolas family spotted her, sailed over the sound and ferried her back. She had a meal at the house, then walked another three miles to the house in Vatersay Township where she lodged. The route on foot to the sound was a recognised one, but getting across depended on attracting the attention of someone on the other side! During the war an assistant teacher was sometimes late for school after returning from Barra via this route having been to a dance in Castlebay the night before – the headmaster, Joseph Campbell, disapprovingly recorded her late arrival on various occasions in the school log book.

There is a very visible legacy of the Second World War in Vatersay, in the form of wreckage from an aircraft. A Catalina flying boat was on a training flight from Oban on the night of 12 May 1944 with nine crew. They were heading for Barra Head where they were going to change course, but due to a faulty compass the plane flew too far north. The navigator realised the error and the pilot began to climb immediately, but it was too late: the plane crashed near the summit of Theiseabhal Beag. There was no fire, and remarkably, six of the nine crew survived. The Barra lifeboat brought the dead and injured to Castlebay. The wreckage was taken down to the shore west of Beanachan and most of it was removed, but some bits were left behind. Parts of wing panels and the tailplane remain to this day, below the road. A memorial was erected at the site in 2007. The Catalina, serial JX273, was one of 200 ordered by the RAF from Boeing in Vancouver, and was destined for service in Africa or India. The crew were from 302 Flying Training Unit based at Oban.[6]

Vatersay lost two of its own men in the war, both of them in the merchant navy.

After the war, dissatisfaction with Vatersay's limitations and lack of basic facilities became more openly voiced, and campaigning for these was to dominate the next forty years. *The Scotsman* of 31 October 1946 reported: 'The 160 inhabitants of Vatersay are threatening to leave the island unless government help is received in the provision of a satisfactory water supply and improved roads.' The threat was exaggerated, either by the source of the story or by the reporter, but the issues were real. The water supply was the original 1909 system of a standpipe or well per township or group of houses, and, incredibly, this system remained until 1974. There were no roads suitable for motor vehicles, only the old track from the jetty at Uidh to the machair beyond Gortein, and the paths to Caolas and Caraigrigh. The track to Gortein from Uidh stopped at the machair – to get to Vatersay Township you walked along the machair or the beach. Eorasdail never got a path at all. Construction of a road from the jetty at Uidh towards Gortein began in 1950, and the sections to Vatersay, Caolas and Caraigrigh were completed five years later. The first tractor had been imported after the war; before then horses had been used for ploughing in south Vatersay, and in the north, where the crofts were much more rough and rocky, spades were used.

The Rev. Ewen MacInnes of Castlebay wrote in 1950 that there was an intention to build a larger jetty at Uidh and to run a daily ferry to Castlebay. The only regular communication was via the post boat run by Allan MacDonald, financed by an annual collection among the islanders. He recorded the resident population as 154, and forty-one working away. Most of these were men working at sea. There were forty-one houses. Thirty children were at the school, and five attended Castlebay Junior Secondary School. They had to stay with relatives in Barra during the week because there was no ferry for them. The priest held Mass every third Sunday and heard confessions the evening before. The islanders would attend Our Lady Star of the Sea at Castlebay on the other Sundays.[7]

In common with the islands in general, the population continued to drop. Lack of job opportunities and poor living standards drove young people to work at sea or on the mainland. Until 1975, Vatersay was a remote and neglected corner of Inverness-shire, and the County Council was reluctant to spend money on marginal communities which, it considered, would soon be abandoned like so many others had been. The population of the small island of Scarp, off Harris, for instance, was dwindling and the last people left in 1971. At a meeting of officials of the Scottish Development Department in Edinburgh in 1964, options for such communities, including Vatersay, were discussed, and evacuation was among them. This was not made public at the time, but emerged about six years later. It was not considered an option by the people who lived there, but it showed how radically things had changed in the islands. Less than sixty years before, a croft on Vatersay was a dream for which the raiders were prepared to sacrifice everything. The raiders from Mingulay had abandoned that island because of its remoteness and lack of facilities, but in the meantime expectations and living standards had risen, and Vatersay was in danger of going the way of Mingulay. The raider generation had settled there in order to escape much worse conditions in Barra and Mingulay, but the generations which had grown up in Vatersay did not have the same attitude to it. Paid employment was more attractive to younger people than crofting, but with few jobs, no shop apart from the post office (there had been four shops in the 1920s), no ferry and poor living standards, there was little to keep them on the island.[8]

Elizabeth Campbell returned to teach in Vatersay in 1966 and found that much had changed in thirty years. Pupil numbers were down to ten, and the island population was down to about ninety. Morale was low, and Vatersay was referred to in newspapers as 'the dying island'. The last inhabitant of the township of Eorasdail had recently left because of its remoteness. It had been the least popular township when applications for crofts were invited in 1909, and in the early years there was a high turnover amongst the tenants of the eight crofts. The last new house was built in 1936, by James MacNeil. Eorasdail was left out of the 1950s road scheme, just as it had been left out of the earlier footpath and jetty schemes. In the later years only older people remained. In a way, it was a warning of what might happen to the whole island.

The islanders realised that they had to take action to halt further population decline and decay, and in 1968 set up their own Council of Social Service. Their first campaign was for a barge to transport cattle to Barra. Hitherto cattle had had to swim across the narrowest part of the sound behind boats, four at a time, their heads held out of the water by men in the boats. The Highlands and Islands Development Board provided a barge. Mains electricity arrived in 1968 and mains water in 1974, from a source in Barra. This was too late for two young children who died in a house fire two years earlier, a tragedy which, had there been a piped water supply, might have been averted. Commenting on the delays in the provision of the water supply, Rev. Calum MacLennan of Castlebay said, 'If we were to accept all the arguments about spending so much money on so few people, then we in the islands might as well pack up and go.'

The first passenger ferry, which ran on request only, started in 1968. It was an open boat owned by Hector MacLeod. The piers at Uidh and Castlebay were unsatisfactory and could only be used at high tide. At other times passengers had to scramble over seaweed-covered rocks or along the seaweed-covered girders of Castlebay pier.[9]

The later 1970s were good times for Vatersay, thanks largely to the more positive attitude to remote communities of the new Western Isles Islands Council (Comhairle nan Eilean Siar), inaugurated in 1975. The first regular ferry service from Barra began in the summer of 1975, when a landing-craft style vessel was bought by the Council. This could carry a vehicle, and a simple slipway was constructed on the sheltered eastern shore of Caolas. At the Castlebay end, a jetty at Ledag had to be used. When carrying passengers only, the landing place at Uidh continued to be used, except at low tide when it could not be approached. The ferry was named by the Vatersay Community Association, A' Bhirlinn Bhatarsach, 'The Vatersay Birlinn', the 'birlinn' being the medieval galley of the islands.

Many of the original houses built in the years after 1909 when the settlement was established were in very poor condition by the 1970s and were not worth renovating. Western Isles Islands

Council therefore built ten wooden bungalows at Vatersay Township in 1975–76. Some old and unoccupied houses were demolished to make way for them. The council declined pleas for houses at Caolas, so Michael Gillies, who lived in a caravan there with a large family, built his own. He called it Gaire an Mara, 'Laughter of the Sea'. The council eventually built three houses at Caolas in 1980.

These developments led to a new spirit of optimism, and this was given a boost in 1977 when a nationwide job creation programme was launched and provided the opportunity to make further improvements. Local people were employed to build a new jetty in 1978–79 about a kilometre (half a mile) west of the old one at Uidh. Although this was a deep water jetty, enabling boats to use it at any state of the tide, it was not designed to be used by a vehicle ferry. The 1975 vessel had been withdrawn after two years as it was unsuitable in many ways, and was replaced by a regular passengers-only service, which at least allowed older children to commute to school in Castlebay daily. Several families had returned to Vatersay because of the new job opportunities, and by 1978 the population reached 111 having been seventy-seven in 1971. There were nineteen children at the school, and another eleven commuted to Castlebay. A coopera- tive shop and café were built at the new jetty, although the building was subsequently damaged by fire. A community hall was built in 1977 on the site of the present hall. Community events had previously taken place in the school. Boats for lobster fishing were bought with help from the Highlands and Islands Development Board. Roy Towers wrote in *The Glasgow Herald* of 4 December 1978: 'The renaissance of Vatersay is a modern miracle of the islands and most remarkable of all, it is a miracle wrought by the islanders themselves'.[10] Rev. Angus MacQueen, priest of Castlebay, was living in Vatersay at the time and was much involved in these developments.

The renaissance didn't last. The job creation schemes finished, and people drifted away. The population fell from 107 in 1981 to 65 in 1988. Decay set in again and there was talk of evacuation. The press got hold of the fact that there were a large number of single young men on the island – eighteen bachelors between the ages of eighteen and forty in 1986 – but not one unmarried woman in the same age group. The following year there was more publicity: a bull supplied by the Department of Agriculture to service Vatersay's cows – 'Bernie' as he was called by the press – drowned while being towed from Vatersay to Barra across the sound. The cattle barge had been withdrawn for safety reasons and was not replaced.

The 1980s also saw a successful campaign for the lifeline link to Barra. In the late 1970s there was talk of a car ferry or a bridge or a causeway over the narrowest part of the sound at Caolas, and building a road on the Barra side from Nask to the crossing point. This was the dream of Elizabeth Campbell: a bridge to Barra, with a link road to Nask along the route she used to walk, and young families returning to the island. She had got involved in the struggle to revitalise the island and was awarded the MBE for services to Vatersay in 1977. Sadly she didn't live to see her dream come true. A proposal for a causeway was submitted to Western Isles Council in 1982. It was approved by the Council in 1984 and by the Scottish Office two years later. The 'Bernie' and bachelors cases highlighted the need for the causeway at a time when arguments were raging about its funding. There were also cases of Vatersay people being drowned while crossing to or from Barra in small boats. By this time Vatersay was the only small inhabited island in the Outer Hebrides which did not have a car ferry.

Construction of the causeway and the link road on Barra began in 1989 and was completed in 1991. The causeway was built of rock blasted from the Barra side. A slipway for boats was provided on each side at the Caolas end, giving access to what had become the lochs on either side of the solid barrier. It is 250 metres long and the minimum depth of water is eleven metres. The final cost was £3.7m, shared between the Scottish Office, Western Isles Council and the European Development Fund. The causeway was the first of the fixed links to the remaining small inhabited islands in the Outer Hebrides. Scalpay (Harris), Berneray (North Uist), and Eriskay (South Uist), were all connected to their larger neighbours by 2001.[11]

The causeway led to another renaissance, or rather transformation, which this time was to be long term. There was a lot of building activity in the following years: new houses were built, and old or ruinous houses were renovated or rebuilt. Several new houses sprang up at Caraigrigh on the Uidh peninsula facing Castlebay, where the old houses had been deserted. For the first time it was possible for people (those who did not have their own boat, anyway) to live in Vatersay and have a full-time job in Barra, not to mention doing things which elsewhere were taken for granted, such as getting shopping without various stages of manhandling, attending social events, going to the doctor and so on. The population rose from seventy-two in 1991 to ninety-four in 2001, and in 2007 it was about 100. The roads have been improved. A new hall was built in 1997 on the site of the old one, which, although only twenty years old, had deteriorated to such an extent that it was not economic to repair it. More recently (2007) renovations were undertaken at the church, previous refurbishment work having been done, inside and out, in 1987–88. A casualty of the causeway was the school: it closed on 17 June 1994, at which time there were only four pupils, three of them from one family. Thereafter they were bussed to school in Castlebay with the older pupils attending the secondary school. The school building is now privately owned and part of it is let as self-catering accommodation. A less tangible down side of the causeway has been some loss of independence and autonomy, but this is accepted as a small price to pay for a secure future.

A great success story in recent years has been the ceilidh band 'The Vatersay Boys'. The band began as Michael and Andy Campbell of Vatersay playing at dances and ceilidhs in Vatersay and Barra. They are great-grandsons of raiders Duncan Campbell and Donald MacIntyre, and sons of melodeon player D.D. (Donald Duncan) Campbell. In 1999 they were joined by the three other members making up the present line-up. They play traditional tunes in modern style, and live performances are particularly popular. In a reviewer's words, 'they have taken the Scottish traditional music scene by storm.'

Crofting, based mainly on cattle and sheep, continues as a part-time occupation for many Vatersay people and there is a healthy demand for crofts. Crofting remains a subject of debate and controversy nationally. Some of the proposals in the proposed Crofting Reform Bill, such as introducing a free market in tenancies, threatened the very foundations of the crofting system and would have been unthinkable to the raiders. The proposed bill was abandoned in 2007. There was controversy in Vatersay itself in 2006 when a croft in Caolas was not assigned to any of the local people keen to get a croft.

Sandray became the focus of attention in 2005 when it was revealed that it and the island of Fuday, off the north-east coast of Barra, were on a list of possible sites for dumping nuclear waste underground. The list had been compiled by the government's nuclear waste disposal agency, Nirex, in the late 1980s. There were detailed plans for a harbour on the east coast of Sandray and a large area inland would be affected by construction work for that and the underground storage facilities. This is the area of shifting sand where there is evidence of human occupation over thousands of years. A construction camp would occupy Gortein MicPhail on the north coast. The islands were chosen because the geology, Lewisian gneiss, is stable and because the islands are uninhabited and far from large centres of population where more opposition might be expected than in sparsely populated areas. Sandray, like Vatersay, is still owned by the Department of Agriculture for Scotland, and is used for the grazing of sheep by the crofters of the township of Vatersay. Nirex maintained that the list was obsolete, but there was swift and strenuous opposition from the people of Barra and Vatersay, and from Western Isles Council and Highland Council. In 2007 the Scottish Government announced its opposition to deep storage facilities in Scotland.[12]

Far from being regarded as suitable as a dumping ground for nuclear waste, Sandray should be cherished and protected. Its cultural heritage is of exceptional interest, since the remains of past human settlement and activity have remained largely unchanged since the eviction of its native population in 1835, and shifting sands are revealing past land surfaces and occupation levels. The three islands to the south have various conservation designations: Mingulay and Berneray are Sites of Special Scientific Interest and Special Protection Areas, mainly on account of their seabird populations, and they and Pabbay have scheduled ancient monuments. The three islands have been owned by the National Trust for Scotland since 2000, and there is a strong case for Sandray's heritage to be recognised.

The story of Vatersay illustrates many aspects of Highland and Island history from the earliest times down to the present day, and the raiding and settlement in the early years of the twentieth century are the most notable aspect of the story. The subsequent history of Vatersay reflects the changing social and economic trends in the Outer Hebrides, particularly the small islands, and the changing attitudes of the state to such communities. At the time of the creation of the crofting settlement, and for many years after, crofting and fishing were the mainstays of the economy of the islands. After the Second World War the problems of communications with Barra, employment, and provision of basic services such as a water supply and electricity became acute. The dwindling population was considered too small to make such services economic, and the Vatersay community was expected to follow other remote communities and die. Through its own efforts and the changing attitudes of the state, the community ensured this did not happen. These efforts culminated in the causeway, and the Vatersay community, founded by the raiders, has a secure and stable future.

References

Note: to keep reference numbers to a minimum, numbers at the end of paragraphs give references for that paragraph, and in some cases, previous paragraphs. References are not given where the source is given in the text.

Abbreviations

CEBB Comunn Eachdraidh Bharraigh agus Bhatarsaigh
CNES Comhairle nan Eilean Siar
CPL Castlebay Public Library
GROS General Register Office for Scotland
NA National Archives
NAS National Archives of Scotland
NLS National Library of Scotland
NMS National Museum of Scotland
NRA National Register of Archives
PP Parliamentary Papers
SAU St Andrews University

SCA Scottish Catholic Archives
SPL Stornoway Public Library
SSS School of Scottish Studies

Chapter 1 Early times

1. Gilbertson et al. 1996, chs 7 and 8; *The Inverness Courier* 10.12.1845
2. All above from Branigan and Foster 2000 and 2002; Branigan 2005 and 2007; Gilbertson et al. 1996 and 1999; RCAHMS 1928
3. Stahl 1999 and 2006. I am indebted to Dr Stahl for assistance with place-names. The Martin story: Nan MacKinnon in SSS: SA/1974.183
4. Branigan 2005; Branigan and Foster 2000

Chapter 2 Tacksmen, landlords, tenants, 1549–1850

1. Cille Mhoire: named in GROS: register of deaths, Barra, 1855–60; NAS: AF42/5369, report on Vatersay. Cille Bhrianain: RCAHMS 1928, 137; Branigan & Foster 2002, 115; Gilbertson et al, 1996, 105–6; Nan MacKinnon: SSS: SA/1974.183. The sand in the vicinity of Sandray's chapel began to drift after the last shepherd who lived a short distance to the north west and had kept the machair in good order died in 1904; NAS AF42/8598. 1915 chapel reference: RCAHMS 1928, 137
2. Nan MacKinnon in *Tocher* 38; MacGregor 1929, 180; www.isleofbarra.com
3. *The Inverness Courier* 3.10.1845
4. 'Barra in 1840' in Campbell (ed) 1936, 200
5. Buxton 1995, 50–51
6. Buxton 1995, 116; Giblin 1964
7. *PP*1895 XXXIX, 924; Beannachan: Nan MacKinnon in SSS: SA/1974.183
8. Buxton 1995, 51
9. Donald MacNeil: Campbell 2000, 96; quote: Campbell 1999, 38; Sandray: MacDonald 1937, 49; Campbell 1992, 88–92
10. Pre-1850 houses: some recorded in Branigan & Foster 2000, others on OS 1880. Barra housing: Branigan 2000
11. 12. NLS: Acc.10688 letter 21.12.1909; Branigan & Foster 2000, 53
12. McKay 1980, 87, 88; MacQueen 1794 in Campbell (ed) 1936
13. Maps: eg Bowen 1776; Thomson 1823; registers: NAS: RH21/50/1
14. Kelp: Walker, in MacKay 1980, 87; Branigan & Foster 2000, 43; crofting: MacCulloch, in Campbell (ed) 1936, 108; Newby 2000, 121
15. Iona: Branigan 2005, ch.9 & app.2; Buxton 1995, 161

16. Rents: Walker (1764) in MacKay 1980, 85; NAS: CS44/446

17. NAS: CS44/446; NAS: RH21/50/1; Thomson 1823

18. NAS: RH21/50/4; Campbell (ed) 1936, 78, 210; Harvie-Brown & Buckley 1888, 177; NMS: letter 17.10.1892

19. The park: Campbell (ed) 1936, 169, 173

20. Campbell (ed) 1936, 96

21. Branigan 2005, 139–141; Campbell (ed) 1936, 187

22. Campbell (ed) 1936, 186

23. Buxton 1995, 160; Branigan and Foster 2000, 65–81; Branigan 2005, 62–66

24. Branigan 2005, 145–46; Campbell 1999, 49; Mrs MacNeil mentioned in estate sale advertisement, *The Scotsman* 8.4.1837

25. NAS: RH21/50/1; NAS: CS 46/4274; Branigan 2005, 38–40; sheep seizure: *PP*1884 XXX111, 666

26. *PP*1895 XXXIX, 920

27. Branigan 2005, 32–36, 141–42; NLS Acc.10706/93; *PP*1895 XXXIX, 933

28. NAS: CS 46/4274; Branigan 2005, 147

29. Buxton 1995, 39–40; SSS: SA1974/107 (Nan MacKinnon)

30. Branigan 2005, ch.8; Richards 1982, ch.13

31. Bulloch 1911, 31–40; Newby 2000, 137–38; NLS: acc.10688, letters 19.6.1909, 24.6.1909, 26.6.1909

32. GROS: register of deaths, Barra parish

Chapter 3 Farm and shipwreck, 1850–1900

1. Thomson map (1823) marks buildings in the area of Vatersay House and farm, but the map's accuracy is uncertain

2. *PP*1854 LX; Charnley 1992

3. Gray's official report (NA: MT9/29/W3747/1866) was published in *PP*1867 LXVI. His much longer confidential report from which most of these quotes are taken is NA: MT9/153/1878 (parts also published in *PP*1867 LXVI). I am indebted to Michael Clark who located the report (Clark 2006)

4. 1887 account: *John o'Groat Journal* 8.6.1887; memorial: NMRS, Vatersay box; map: NAS: RHP44187

5. Other claims relating to salvage are in NAS: GD403/29/1–14; official report: *PP*1854 LX; 1887 account: *John o'Groat Journal* 8.6.1887

6. Aftermath of Gray's reports and article: *PP*1867 LXVI

7. K. Gillies: SSS: SA1960/94, also in SA1974/109 (Nan MacKinnon); MacGregor 1929, 172–73. Some details of wrecks from Lloyds List, National Maritime Museum

8. *The Glasgow Herald* 18.7.08 'The Barra Raiders'; rats: NMS: letter 17.11.1888

9. NAS: RHP44187

10. NAS: AF17/155, 156; 1887 account: *John o'Groat Journal* 8.6.1887; 1892 failure: NMS: letter 17.10.1892

11. SPL: article in unnamed newspaper

12. Bulloch 1911; *PP*1895 XXXIX, 931–3, 942; *PP*1884 XXX111, 650; GROS: 1891 census; sales advertised in *The Scotsman*

13. CPL: Castlebay School Log Book; CNES: Minute book of Barra School Board, 1888–1918; plan: NAS: AF42/7098. Neil McCuish was recorded as a scholar in the 1901 census, but in the admissions register of the new school he was said to have never attended school when he started there in 1910, aged fourteen.

Chapter 4 Early raids, 1900–1906

1. Huts: *PP*1895 XXXIX, 941

2. *PP*1895 XXXIX , 932–3; *PP*1884 XXX111, 653, 655, 683–96; Storrie 1962

3. *PP*1895 XXXIX, 943–44; Cameron 1996 109–10

4. NAS: AF67/122 police report 15.3.01; Hunter 1976, 188; Cameron 1997, 50. The potato arrangement may have begun before 1900: see Cameron 1996, 110

5. NAS: AF67/120 police reports

6. NAS: AF67/120 police reports

7. NAS: AF67/121 police reports

8. NAS: AF67/122 police reports; *PP* 1908 LXXXVIII, hereafter referred to as *Vatersay Correspondence*, 36

9. NAS: AF67/123, 130, police reports

10. NAS: AF67/130; AF42/1467,1549,1550

11. NAS: AF67/132; AF42/2412; *Vatersay Correspondence* 36–37; Campbell: *PP*1895 XXXIX, 928

12. *Vatersay Correspondence*, 38

13. NAS: AF67/132; AF42/2280; Day 1918

14. NAS: AF42/2887

15. NAS: AF42/2996

16. NAS: AF42/2910

17. NAS: AF42/2996

18. NAS: AF67/132 police reports

19. NAS: AF67/132; *Vatersay Correspondence* 22–25, 32

20. *Vatersay Correspondence*, 24

21. NAS: AF67/132

Chapter 5 The invasion, 1906–1907

1. NAS: AF67/134 police reports; *Vatersay Correspondence*, 3
2. NAS: AF67/134 police reports; Cameron 1996, 112
3. *Vatersay Correspondence*, 32–33
4. NAS: AF67/134 police reports
5. NAS: AF67/134 police report 12.11.1906 (Campbell)
6. Buxton 1995 and 2005; 1901 census (in which John MacKinnon, builder of the gabled house in the village, lived in a three-roomed house, presumably the new one); R. MacNeil: SSS SA1960/96
7. NAS: AF67/134 police reports; NAS: AF42/3674 ('invasion' quote)
8. NAS: CS241/889/1; NAS: AF67/134 police reports
9. SSS: SA1960/103, recorded and translated by Lisa Storey, to whom I am indebted. Michael MacPhee talked about the raids on SSS: SA1960/92, see Storey 2007, 149–53
10. Report in *Vatersay Correspondence*, 33–36; NAS: AF42/5369; NAS: AF67/136
11. *Parliamentary Debates* 6.8.1907
12. *The Scotsman* 29.1.1908
13. *Vatersay Correspondence*, 4; Cameron 1996, 114
14. *Vatersay Correspondence*, 6–7
15. NAS: NRA, Skene, Edwards and Garson TD85/63/A8/13, letters 25.11.1900, 22.1.1901; Cameron 1996, 91, 95; *Vatersay Correspondence*, 5
16. *Vatersay Correspondence*, 7–10, 16–21; Cameron 1996, 117
17. NAS: AF67/134, 135, 137 (18.7.08); AF42/3980; *Vatersay Correspondence*, 6; Cameron 1996, 103–109 (Kilmuir)
18. NAS: AF67/135 police reports; AF42/8598; *The Glasgow Herald* 18.7.1908. In 1883 Sandray was used for grazing by Eoligarry Farm, *PP*1895 XXXIX, 933

Chapter 6 The trial, 1908

1. NAS: CS241/888, 889; *Vatersay Correspondence*, 32–33
2. NAS: AF67/137 police reports; Buxton 1995
3. NLS: Acc.10688 letter 23.3.1908
4. NAS: AF42/5494
5. *The Scotsman* 27.5.1908
6. Petitions: NAS: AF67/136, 137
7. NAS: NRA TD85/63/A8/18 'Further correspondence . . .'; *The Scotsman* 20.5.09; *Vatersay Correspondence*, 8
8. *The Glasgow Herald* 18.7.1908

Chapter 7 Purchase and division, 1908–9

1. NAS: AF67/137 police reports; AF42/5318, 5369, 5494
2. The meeting: NLS: Acc.10688 letter 12.7.1908; Kentangaval applicants: NAS: AF42/5369
3. NAS: AF42/5269
4. NAS: AF42/5369
5. NAS: NRA TD85/63/A8/19 'Further correspondence . . .'; AF42/5839; Cameron 1996, 115–17
6. Cameron 1996, 117
7. Letter to Sinclair: NAS: AF67/142 letter 27.7.1908; consultation: NLS: Acc.10688 letter 24.3.09; NAS: AF42/5369, report on Vatersay
8. NAS: AF42/5369, report on Vatersay
9. NAS: AF42/5529, 5641
10. NAS: AF42/5369, report on Vatersay; AF42/6002,3,4,5; NAS: RHP5237/1, map. According to Nan MacKinnon, in former times the settlement at what is now the township of Vatersay was in two parts, Scarp, and an Uigh, SSS: SA/1974.183
11. NAS: AF42/5369, report on Vatersay; SSS: SA/1960.92, Michael MacPhee
12. NAS: AF42/5989
13. NLS: Acc.10688 letter 19.5.1909
14. application form: NAS: AF42/6111; comments: NAS: AF42/5494, 5318
15. NAS: AF42/6209, 6210
16. NAS: AF42/6320, 6321, 6421, 6592, 6694
17. NLS: Acc.10688 letter 19.6.1909
18. Campbell (ed) 1936, 274–75
19. NAS: AF42/6273
20. NLS: Acc.10688 letter 26.6.1909
21. NAS: AF42/6210, 6273
22. NAS: AF42/6475 (both letters)
23. NAS: AF42/6320, 6501, 6582
24. NLS: Acc.10688 letter 26.6.1909
25. NAS: AF42/6501, 6582, 6686, 6739; AF67/370
26. NLS: Acc.10688 letter 11.10.1909; NAS: AF42/6768, 6689. MacPhee was probably the author of a letter on the subject in *The Scotsman* of 7.9.1909 signed by 'Hebridean'.
27. MacPhees: NAS: AF67/370; MacLean: NAS: AF42/9552 and family knowledge
28. NAS: AF42/5380, 5369; AF67/137
29. CDB order: NAS: AF42/5990
30. Buxton 1995, 98–99

Chapter 8 Establishing the community, 1910–1913

1. The resisters: *The Glasgow Herald* 1.1.1910; NAS: AF42/6649, 6665. H MacKinnon: NAS: AF42/6302, 5369
2. *Tocher* 38, 1983, 6
3. NAS: AF42/6302
4. NAS: AF42/7071, 7198, 7323, 7327, 7661, 7667, 7981
5. NAS: AF42/7956, 8263, 8512, 8559
6. *Tocher* 38, 1983, 6–7
7. NAS: AF42/6650, 6916, 7158, 7176, 7873, 8106, 9599
8. NAS: AF42/6410, 7158
9. NAS: AF42/6676, 7098
10. NAS: AF42/6901, 6930; NLS: Acc.10688 letter 24.1.1912
11. NAS: AF42/6676
12. NAS: AF42/7425, 8772, 9114
13. NAS: AF42/9472, 9544; NLS: Acc.10688 letter 5.6.1909
14. NAS: AF42/9472
15. NLS: Acc.10688 letter 7.3.1911
16. NAS: AF42/7911, 8983, 9340
17. NAS: AF42/5369; *The Inverness Courier* 10.12.1845; NLS: Acc.10688 letter 1.4.1911
18. NAS: AF42/9179, 9401, 9499
19. NAS: AF42/7640, 8176; NLS: Acc.10688 letter 14.8.1911
20. Buxton 1995, ch.13; NAS: AF42/7629
21. Buxton 1995 ch.13; NAS: AF42/7384, 7533, 9598; Vatersay School Admission Register
22. Buxton 1995, ch.13, app.2; M. Campbell: SSS: SA1960/92
23. NAS: AF42/6588, 6676, 6681, 7129
24. CPL: Vatersay School Log Book, 1910–1994; School Admission Register
25. Buxton 1995; NAS: AF42/7197, 7947, 8181, 8848; Vatersay School Admission Register
26. CPL: Vatersay School Log Book, 1910–1994
27. NAS: AF42/7098
28. Local knowledge; *Scottish Catholic Directory* 1914–1915. Funding: no record in Bute archives. Benches: it is uncertain whether they include those from Mingulay chapel

Chapter 9 Since the raiders

1. *Idomeneus*: www.red-duster.co.uk, www.isleofvatersay.com; *Aranda*: *The Scotsman* 30.5.1917, MacGregor 1929, 173; local knowledge. *Aranda* appears in Adam photographs (SAU)
2. CPL: Vatersay School Log Book

3. Tenders for demolition invited in *The Scotsman* 18.1.1930
4. *The Scotsman* 27.11.1920 and subsequently; NAS: VR103; local knowledge
5. *The Scotsman* 22.7.1935; Gordon 1941; Campbell and Collinson 1969
6. *Guth Bharraidh* 8.2.2002
7. SCA: DA42/107/1
8. SDD meeting: *The Scotsman* 25.12.1970
9. Chaimbeul 1982; ferry: *The Scotsman* 21.10.1968, Brian Wilson in *West Highland Free Press* 21.9.1973; fire and MacLennan quote: *West Highland Free Press* 1.12.1972
10. Chaimbeul 1982; *The Scotsman* 5.9.1975; Roy Towers in *The Glasgow Herald* 4.12.1978; Peter Dunn in *The Independent Weekend* 24.9.1988; Cooper 1985, ch.12
11. Royle et al 1990; www.w-isles.gov.uk/eriskay/vatersay; Riddoch 2007, 21–26
12. An attempt by a developer to buy land to build holiday accommodation at Caraigrigh was fought off by the islanders on the basis that it was crofting land; *Guth Bharraidh* 11.6.1993. Sandray: David Ross in *The Herald* 11.6.2005; http://critics.sundayherald.com/downloads/nirex/map_Redcar.pdf; *Guth Bharraidh* 27.6.2007

Bibliography

Blaeu, Joan 1654: map of Scotland derived from Timothy Pont, late 16th century.

Blundell, Odo (1917), *The Catholic Highlands of Scotland* (London, Sands & co).

Bowen, Thomas (1776), *The south part of Long Island from Bara Head to Benbecula* (map) (London, MacKenzie).

Branigan, Keith (2005), *From clan to clearance, history and archaeology on the Isle of Barra c.850–1850* AD (Oxford, Oxbow Books).

Branigan, Keith (2007), *Ancient Barra*, Comhairle nan Eilean Siar.

Branigan, Keith and Foster, Patrick (2000) *From Barra to Berneray: archaeological research and excavation in the southern isles of the Outer Hebrides* (Sheffield, Sheffield Academic Press).

Branigan, Keith and Foster, Patrick (2002), *Barra and the Bishop's Isles, living on the margin* (Stroud, Tempus).

Branigan, Keith, and Merrony, Colin (2000), 'The Hebridean blackhouse on the Isle of Barra', *Scottish Archaeological Journal* 22, pp. 1–16.

Buchanan, Donald (1942), *Reflections of the Isle of Barra* (London, Sands & Co.).

Bulloch, John M. (1911), *The Gordons of Cluny* (privately published).

Buxton, Ben (1995), *Mingulay, an island and its people* (Edinburgh, Birlinn).

Buxton, Ben (2006), 'The decline and fall of Mingulay' in *The decline and fall of St Kilda* published by The Islands Book Trust, Port of Ness. Reprinted in the Trust's *Island Notes* series.

Cameron, Ewen A. (1996), *Land for the people? The British Government and the Scottish Highlands, c.1880–1925* (East Linton, Tuckwell Press).

Cameron, Ewen A. (1997), 'They will listen to no remonstrance': land raids and land raiders in the Scottish Highlands, 1886–1914', *Scottish Economic & Social History* 17, pp. 43–64.

Cameron, James (1912), *The old and the new Highlands and Hebrides* (Kirkcaldy, Cameron). Written 1910.

Campbell, J.L., ed. (1936), *The Book of Barra* (London, G. Routledge).

—— ed. (1992), *Tales from Barra Told by The Coddy (John MacPherson, Northbay, Barra, 1876–1955)*, (Edinburgh, Birlinn).

—— (1999), *Songs Remembered in Exile: traditional Gaelic songs from Nova Scotia recorded in Cape Breton and Antigonish County in 1937 with an account of the causes of the Highland Emigration, 1790–1835* (2nd edn, Edinburgh, Birlinn). Includes historical background to 19th-century emigrations from Barra.

—— (2000) *A very civil people: Hebridean folk, history and tradition* (Edinburgh, Birlinn).

—— and Collinson, F. (1981), *Hebridean Folksongs 3. Waulking songs from Vatersay, Barra, Eriskay, South Uist and Benbecula* (Oxford, Clarendon Press).

Catholic Directory, dates indicated in references.

Chaimbeul, Ealasaid (1982), *Air Mo Chuairt* (Stornoway, Acair).

Charnley, Bob (1992), *Shipwrecked on Vatersay!* (Broadford, MacLean Press).

Clark, Michael (2006), 'Shipwrecks and Barra', *History Scotland* 6 no. 6, pp. 24–28, and (2007) 7 no. 7, pp. 36–39.

Collinson, Francis (1961), 'The musical aspect of the songs of Nan MacKinnon of Vatersay' *Scottish Studies* 5, pp. 40–42.

Comunn Eachdraidh Bharraigh agus Bhatarsaigh (CEBB), 1993: *Tales, Songs, Tradition, from Barra and Vatersay* (re Nan MacKinnon, reproduced from *Tocher* 38), Castlebay.

Cooper, Derek (1985), *The Road to Mingulay: a view of the Western Isles* (London, Routledge & Kegan Paul).

Day, J.P. (1918), *Public Administration in the Highlands and Islands of Scotland* (London).

The Edinburgh Evening News, details given in references.

Gaelic Schools Society: *Annual Reports* 1811–1845 (Edinburgh, Gaelic Schools Society). Barra sections reproduced in J.L. Campbell, ed., 1936.

Giblin, C., ed. (1964), *The Irish Franciscan Mission to Scotland, 1619–1646: documents from Roman archives* (Dublin, Assisi Press).

Gilbertson, David, Kent M., Grattan, J. (1996), *The Outer Hebrides, the last 14,000 years* (Sheffield, Sheffield Academic Press).

Gilbertson, D.D., J.-L. Schwenninger, R.A. Kemp, E.J. Rhodes (1999), 'Sand drift and soil formation along an exposed North Atlantic coastline: 14,000 years of diverse geomorphological, climatic and human impacts', *Journal of Archaeological Science* 26, pp. 439–69.

The Glasgow Herald/The Herald, details given in references.

Gordon, Seton (1941), 'Isles of the Outer Hebrides', *Scottish Geographical Magazine* 57, 1, pp. 115–19.

Gray, Thomas (1866), 'Barra, in the Outer Hebrides', *Nature and Art*, December, pp. 193–200.

Guth Bharraidh, details given in references.

Harvie-Brown, J. A. and Buckley, T. E. (1888), *A Vertebrate Fauna of the Outer Hebrides* (Edinburgh, Douglas).

Hunter, James (1976), *The Making of the Crofting Community* (Edinburgh, John Donald Publishers).

The Inverness Courier, details given in references.

John o'Groat Journal 1887, 'Notes of a trip to Barra', 25 May, 1&8 June.

MacCulloch, John (1824), *The Highlands and Western Isles of Scotland* (London, Longman, Hurst, Rees, Orme, Brown and Green). Barra sections reproduced in J.L. Campbell, ed. (1936).

MacDonald, J.M. (1937), *Highland Ponies and some Reminiscences of Highland Men* (Stirling,). d/k

MacGregor, Alasdair A. (1929), *Summer Days among the Western Isles* (Edinburgh, Nelson).

MacGregor, Alasdair A. (1958), 'Primrose Isle' *Scotland's Magazine* 54, 2, pp. 38–42.

McKay, Margaret M., ed. (1980), *The Rev. Dr John Walkers Report on the Hebrides of 1764 and 1771* (Edinburgh, John Donald).

MacQueen, Edward (1794), 'Parish of Barray', *Statistical Account of Scotland,* vol. 13, pp. 326–342. Reproduced in J.L. Campbell, ed. (1936).

Martin, Martin (1703), *A Description of the Western Islands of Scotland* (London, Andrew Bell). Barra sections reproduced in J.L. Campbell, ed. (1936).

Monro, Donald, 1774: *A Description of the Western Isles of Scotland called Hybrides* (c.1549), Edinburgh Barra sections reproduced in J.L. Campbell, ed. (1936).

Newby, Andrew (2000), 'Emigration and clearance from the Island of Barra, c1770–1858', *Transactions of the Gaelic Society of Inverness* 61, pp. 116–48.

Nicolson, Alexander (1845), 'Parish of Barray', *New Statistical Account of Scotland,* (Edinburgh). Reproduced in J.L. Campbell, ed. (1936).

The Oban Times, details given in references.

Ordnance Survey: Inverness-shire 1:10,560 map sheets LXVI, LXVII (Vatersay and Sandray), LXIV (N Vatersay) 1st edition 1880 (surveyed 1878), 2nd edition 1904 (surveyed 1901).

Parliamentary Debates 6 August 1907.

Parliamentary Papers 1854 LX: 'Report of an investigation into the loss of the Annie Jane'.

—— 1867 LXIV: 'Wrecking in the Hebrides'.

—— 1884 XXXII–XXXVI: 'Report of Her Majesty's Commissioners of Inquiry into the Condition of the Crofters and Cottars in the Highlands and Islands of Scotland' (The Napier Commission).

—— 1895 XXXVII, XXXIX: 'Royal Commission (Highlands and Islands, 1892)'.

—— 1908 LXXXVIII: 'Return of Correspondence . . . with Reference to the Seizure and Occupation of the Island of Vatersay' (referred to as *Vatersay correspondence* in references).

—— 1908 LXXXVIII: 'Report . . . of the County Council of Inverness upon Applications for Allotments in North Uist and Barra in 1897'.

RCAHMS 1928: *Inventory of Monuments and Constructions in the Outer Hebrides, Skye, and the Small Isles,* Edinburgh.

Richards, Eric (1982), *A History of the Highland Clearances: agrarian transformation and the evictions 1746–1886* (London, Croom Helm).

Riddoch, Lesley (2007), *Riddoch on the Outer Hebrides* (Edinburgh, Luath Press Ltd).

Ross, James (1961), 'Folk song and social environment, a study of the repertoire of Nan MacKinnon of Vatersay', *Scottish Studies* 5, pp. 18–39.

Royle, Stephen, Robinson, A.J., and Smith, B.L. (1990), 'Fixed links in the Western Isles: the Barra-Vatersay causeway', *Scottish Geographical Magazine* 106 no. 2, pp. 117–120.

The Scotsman, details given in references.

Stahl, Anke-Beate (1999), *Place-names of Barra in the Outer Hebrides* (unpublished PhD thesis, University of Edinburgh).

Stahl, Anke-Beate (2006), 'On the verge of loss: lesser known place-names of Barra and Vatersay', in Arne Kruse, ed., *Barra and Skye: two Hebridean perspectives* (Edinburgh, Scottish Society for Northern Studies).

Storey, Lisa (2007), *Muinntir Mhiughalaigh* (Glasgow, Clàr).

Storrie, Margaret (1962), 'Two early resettlement schemes in Barra', *Scottish Studies* 6, pp. 71–84.

School of Scottish Studies Archives (1983), 'Nan MacKinnon', *Tocher* 38, pp. 1–48.

Vatersay correspondence see *Parliamentary Papers* 1908 LXXXVIII.

Walker, John, 1764: see McKay 1980.

West Highland Free Press, details given in references.

Unpublished sources

Castlebay Public Library

Log books of Vatersay School 1910–1994.

Log book of Castlebay School (for Vatersay Sub-School) 1896–1900.

Comhairle nan Eilean Siar

Minute book of Barra School Board 1888–1918.

General Register Office for Scotland

Census enumerators' books, Barra Parish, 1841–1901.

Registers of Births, Marriages, Deaths, Barra Parish, from 1855.

National Archives

MT9/29/W3747/1866: 2 letters by Thomas Gray to Thomas Farrer, 20 August 1866 (one marked 'private and confidential'; the other, the official report) parts of both published in *PP*1867 LXVI.

MT9/153 'Barra and the adjacent islands, confidential notes' by Thomas Gray, 15 September 1866 (filed with MT9/153/M.7215/78).

National Archives of Scotland

AF17: Fishery Board records

AF17/155,156: Stornoway Fisheries Office records from 1868.

AF42: Congested Districts Board records, relating to the raiding and settlement of Vatersay (file numbers given in references).

AF67: Scottish Office Crofting Files relating to the raiding and settlement of Vatersay (file numbers given in references).

CS44/box446: Court of Session. MacNeil's trustees *v* MacDonald's creditors, rental of 1810–11.

CS241/888, 889: Court of Session. Cathcart *v* Campbell and nine others, 1908.

GD403/29/1–14: documents relating to salvage of the *Annie Jane*.

NRA TD85/63/A8/19: 'Further correspondence between Lady Gordon Cathcart and the Secretary for Scotland . . . June 1908–February 1909'.

RH4/23/106: Ordnance Survey Object Name Book, Barra Parish, 1878.

RH21: Roman Catholic Diocese of Argyll and the Isles records. RH21/50/1, 2, 3, registers of baptisms, marriages (and some deaths) (Craigston), 1805–1853. RH21/50/4, account book of Rev Angus MacDonald, Craigston, 1818–22.

RHP 44187: plan of Barra Parish, 1861–63, by Otter and Edye, scale approx. 1:15,000 (Admiralty Chart).

RHP 34134: small-scale version of above, with some locations enlarged.

RHP 5237/1: Ordnance Survey map with proposed crofts, roads, etc., 1909.

VR 103: valuation rolls, Inverness-shire, 1855 onwards.

National Library of Scotland

Acc. 10688: Letterbook of Neil MacPhee of Vatersay, 1909–12 (microfilm copy, access restricted).

Acc. 10706/93: Business Records of Robert Stevenson & Sons, Civil Engineers: Reports on Northern Lighthouses 1830–1837.

National Monuments Record of Scotland

NMRS database of sites.

Royal Museum of Scotland

Harvie-Brown Collection: letters of John Finlayson to Harvie-Brown: 17.11.1888, 17.10.1892.

St Andrews University

Robert M. Adam collection of photographs: Vatersay, July 1922.

School of Scottish Studies

SA1974/109, SA1974/183, SA1974/187: tape recordings of Vatersay people.

SA1981/31, SA1981/35 (Nan MacKinnon).

SA1960/103 (John MacDougall).

SA1960/92 (Michael MacPhee).

SA1960/94 (Kate Gillies).

SA1960/99 (Mary Campbell).

SA1960/96 (Roderick MacNeil).

Scottish Catholic Archives

DA42/107/1: Rev. Ewen MacInnes, Report on Vatersay, 11.7.1950.

DA42/485: Letter concerning church refurbishment 7.12.1987.

Stornoway Public Library

Article from unnamed newspaper: 'About the Hebrides', 1882 or 1883.

In private hands

Admission Register, Vatersay School, 1910–1994.

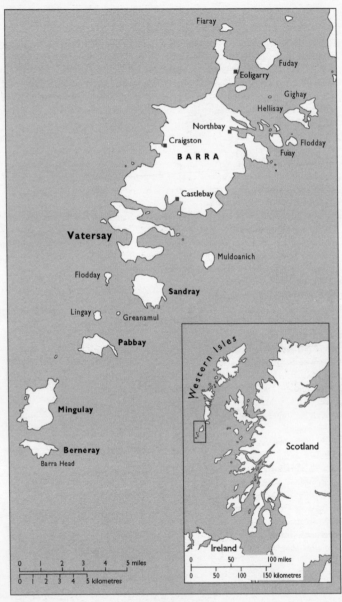

1. The Barra Isles

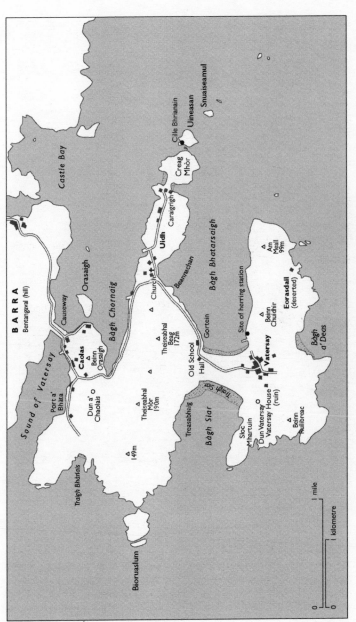

2. Vatersay. The names of the hills in northern Vatersay are as shown on the Ordnance Survey maps, but are known locally as follows: 190m peak, A' Bheinn Mhòr; 149m peak, A' Bheinn Beag; 172m peak, Theiseabhal Mòr; peak to its east, Theiseabhal Beag.

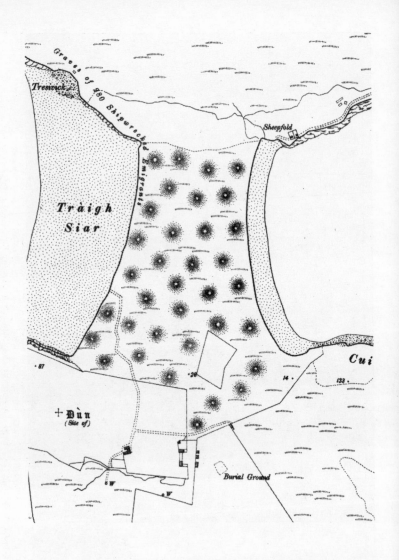

Map labels: *Treswick*, *Graves of 350 Shipwrecked Emigrants*, *Träigh Siar*, *Sheepfold*, *Cui*, *+ Dùn (Site of)*, *Burial Ground*

3. The area around Vatersay House and Farm, from the Ordnance Survey map of 1901. The farm steading is the 'square' of buildings west of the Burial Ground, and Vatersay House is between the steading and the dun. The southern end of the present township of Vatersay is on the site of the steading, and the rest of the township occupies the area to the northeast, where the raiders built their huts in 1906–7. To the north, the two buildings at the Sheepfold were a wool shed and dipper shed.

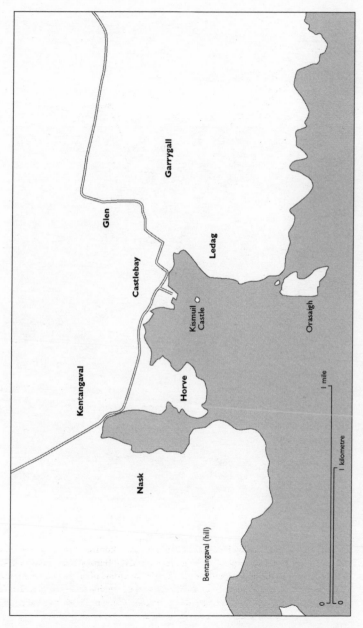

4. Castle Bay, Barra, around 1900, showing the townships where many of the Vatersay Raiders came from.

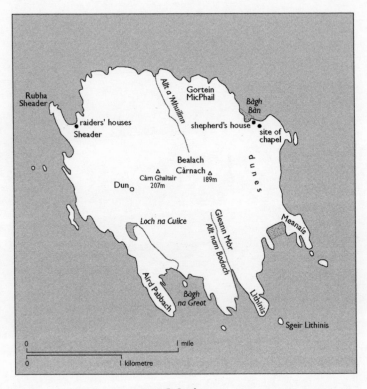

Rubha
Sheader

Alt a 'Mhuilinn

Gortein
MicPhail

Bàgh
Bàn

• raiders' houses
Sheader

shepherd's house •

site of
chapel

Bealach
Càrnach

△
Càrn Ghaltair
207m

△
189m

Dun ○

d u n e s

Loch na Cuilce

Gleann Mòr
Allt nam Bodach

Meanais

Aird Pabbach

Bàgh
na Greot

Lithinis

○ Sgeir Lithinis

0 _____ 1 mile

0 _____ 1 kilometre

5. Sandray

Appendix 1: Chronology of the raiding and settlement, and main people involved

1850   crofters are evicted and Vatersay becomes a single farm
1883   first appeal by Barra cottars for crofts on Vatersay
1886   first recorded seizure of potato ground
1900   September: first of a series of raids up to 1906
1903   January: Congested Districts Board buys potato ground from landowner, Lady Gordon Cathcart
1906   July: the invasion; raiders start settling
1907   January: Mingulay people begin raiding
1907   April: Lady Cathcart serves interdicts on raiders, ordering them to leave
1907   November: Mingulay men raid Sandray
1908   June: the trial; ten raiders sentenced to two months imprisonment
1908   July: Lady Cathcart agrees to create a crofting settlement
1909   February: the government is forced to buy Vatersay and Sandray; invites applications for crofts
1909   May: allocation of crofts; furore over unsuccessful applicants
1910   June: school opens
1911   most of the remaining inhabitants of the islands to the south get crofts
1912   initial allocation of crofts complete; last Mingulay people get crofts
1913   the church is built

Main people involved at the time of the raids

Campbell, Duncan: leader of the Vatersay raiders

Campbell, Michael: leader of the raiders from Mingulay

Cathcart, Lady Gordon: landowner of Vatersay and Sandray, 1878–1909 (and of Barra, 1878–1932)

Dewar, (Sir) John: MP for Inverness-shire from 1905

MacDonald, Donald: tenant farmer of Vatersay and Sandray 1883–1909

MacGregor, R: secretary of the Congested Districts Board

MacPhee, Neil ('senior'; Niall Chaluim): the raiders' public relations man, and ground officer for Vatersay from 1912

Pentland, Lord: *see* Sinclair, John

Shaw, Donald: the raiders' legal agent

Shaw, Thomas: Lord Advocate for Scotland, 1905–1909

Sinclair, John: Secretary for Scotland, 1905–11; became Lord Pentland in 1909

Names of the raiders who were imprisoned, and their legal advisers in plate 7:

Back row left to Right: Arthur Dewar, counsel; John MacDougall; John Sinclair; William Boyd; Donald Shaw, lawyer. Middle row Left to Right: John Campbell; Roderick MacNeil; Duncan Campbell, leader; Donald MacIntyre, Michael Campbell. Front row Left to Right: Duncan Sinclair, Hector MacPhee (see also p. 95).

Appendix 2: Vatersay population figures

Year	Population	Inhabited houses (1841–1921)
1764	104	
1841	84	14
1851	64	8
1861	32	4
1871	17★	2
1881	19	4
1891	32	3
1901	32 ★★	4
1911	288	55
1921	262	58
1931	240	
1946	160	
1951	151	
1961	95	
1969	90	
1971	77	
1978	111	
1981	107	
1985	65	
1991	72	
1993	83	
2001	94	

★ the published figure of 22 included 5 fishermen from Aberdeenshire, in a hut
★★ the published figure of 13 was due to carelessness in recording by the census enumerator

Appendix 3: Nan MacKinnon and oral tradition

Nan MacKinnon of Vatersay (1902–82) became celebrated for her knowledge of Gaelic stories, songs, proverbs and sayings. She was recorded by John Lorne Campbell in 1937, and by various members of staff of the School of Scottish Studies in Edinburgh from 1951 up to 1981.

Nan Eachain Fhionnlaigh was born in Kentangaval, Barra, the youngest child of Hector MacKinnon and Mary MacPhee, who was from Mingulay. Hector was a cottar, and was one of the Vatersay raiders in 1906. He subsequently built a house at Caolas, which the family moved into in 1908. Three years later they moved to Caraigrigh (see chapter 8).

Nan left her home island for some years and worked on the mainland. In 1940 her sister, Kate Flora, died leaving a young family in Vatersay, and their father, Jonathan MacLeod, being away at sea, Nan returned from Glasgow to look after them. She remained in Vatersay for the rest of her life.

From her father she learned sea songs and songs of the 1745 uprising. She inherited most of her knowledge of oral tradition from her mother. Because there was a lot of movement among the communities of the Barra Isles through intermarriage, evictions, and raiding, her inheritance was of the islands as a whole as well as South Uist (via a great-great-grandmother) and further afield. She absorbed it while growing up, and more consciously as an adult, and held it all in her memory. It was all in Gaelic, of course, which she could neither read not write, yet she could read and write fluently in English – education was exclusively in English, and she would have used it when working on the mainland.

Nan was heir to a noble cultural tradition. Collectors of folklore had recorded people in the Barra Isles as early as the 1860s because more oral culture survived there than in other parts of Scotland. This was partly due to their remoteness, and also because the islands had escaped the repressive influence of the Protestant Reformation on oral culture in the islands to the north and most of the rest of Scotland.

The storytelling tradition of Gaelic society is remarkably rich and varied. The stories are of various types: heroic, historical, supernatural. Storytelling was the main occupation during the long winter evenings, when people would gather at someone's house for a ceilidh. At these informal gatherings stories were told mainly by men. Nan recited over 400 stories to James Ross of the School of Scottish Studies and then told him she had as many again in her memory. Long stories could take hours – or even days – to recite.

The singing of song was part of everyday life. There were love songs, songs in praise of people, songs of historical events, and songs of the supernatural. There were work songs to accompany all sorts of rhythmical and repetitive activities – spinning, weaving, waulking (fulling cloth), preparing food, milking, ploughing (with the foot plough or spade), rowing. Singing was not accompanied by musical instruments. The bagpipes, the traditional instrument, accompanied dancing.

Francis Collinson wrote of Nan MacKinnon's singing in 1961:

The singing of Nan MacKinnon has a strangeness about it even to the person with a wide experience of Gaelic folk-singing. One might say facilely of it that it is 'out of this world'. For once, however, the phrase would be justified, for it is the singing of a person who lives, and sings for her own amusement, within the confines of her immediate family circle, in the midst of a small island community which itself chooses to enjoy a withdrawn existence, and where visitors are not encouraged to intrude. Her singing, which is the legacy of her mother, has therefore probably preserved . . . the way of singing of that older island community in which her mother lived the greater part of her life – that of the now uninhabited island of Mingulay.

James Ross wrote in 1961 about his 'major fieldwork project which has culminated in the recording from this singer of what is possibly the greatest individual repertoire ever to be collected.'

Nan MacKinnon lamented the passing of the ceilidh: 'You know the ceilidhs, the day of the ceilidhs and the singing of songs and the telling of stories is gone. Oh, yes, I think it [television] ruined the days of the ceilidhs, and the old stories and the old songs and the waulking songs and all that.'

Television arrived with mains electricity, in 1968.

One of her stories, 'The Gold Ship', was about historical tradition in Vatersay. Here are transcriptions of the English and Gaelic versions of the story recorded in 1981.

The Gold Ship

Once upon a time when the people weren't as advanced as what they are today, a ship came to anchor in the bay at Vatersay here. There weren't many people here. They were the tenants of MacNeil of Barra at the time. It's ages ago. And this ship was in the bay for six months on end. So the people were wondering what was the matter or why weren't they leaving. And they used to come round the houses for eggs, ducks or hens or anything they could get. And it didn't matter how small the item was, supposing it was a dozen eggs or half a dozen, it was a guinea or a sovereign or half a sovereign or half a guinea give for this, and things were very cheap at that time.

Anyway, someone more advanced than the rest sent word away about this mysterious ship that had been anchored in the Vatersay Bay for six months. They had no word of going. They thought there was something mysterious about them. And a sheriff was brought to the island. So the sheriff called them all ashore. And when they used to go around the houses, there was always a fair-haired little boy along with them. And they were all brought ashore.

And he started questioning the little boy first. And the little boy started to cry. 'I can't tell you anything,' he said. 'I was sworn that I wouldn't tell anything. So,' he said, 'I'm afraid of my life. I can't tell you anything.'

'Well,' the sheriff said, 'I'll tell you what, my boy, just you go over to that big boulder over there, and tell the boulder the whole story, what happened.'

And the boy started telling the story. His father was the captain of the ship. And it was a cargo of gold they had coming from Spain. And they thought that if they got rid of the captain, that they would have all this gold to themselves. And after murdering the captain they hadn't the heart to kill the little boy. But they swore him on his oath not to tell what happened. So the little boy told the boulder all that happened, the big boulder. And the sheriff was listening to every word he said. So he told them that they killed his father and that he promised that he wouldn't tell a thing: that he was warned, that he was terrified for his life.

'Oh, well,' the sheriff said, 'My boy, you'll be safe enough from now on. And I'm glad you told the story. And they're not to hurt a hair of your head,' he said. 'You'll be looked after from now on. And you don't need to depend on them.'

And the whole crowd of them was taken away, the whole ship. But the wee boy was kept behind. Whatever happened to them after leaving Vatersay Bay down here nobody in Barra knew. But of course people weren't as advanced as what they are today. If it was today it would be on the radio, that night and the next day and you'd get the whole story afterwards. But in those days things were very slow and I suppose they were sent to jail or they might have been hanged or something. There were some queer doings here. You know, this was an out-of-the-way place and nobody was going to get them but it was just the gold that . . . made them kill the captain. But it didn't do them any good, mind you.

Soitheach an Oir

Thàinig soitheach a bhàgh Bhatarsaigh uair-eigin agus bha i sia mìosan ann gun fhalbh as, 's cha robh fios aig na daoine fon t-saoghal có as an tàinig i 's cha robh i brath air falbh as. Bha an uair sin an t-àite bha seo, bha e, mar a chanadh iad, fo thuath 's bhiodh iad a' tighinn air tìr a dh'iarraidh cearcan 's ag iarraidh tunnagan 's ag iarraidh uighean. Ga brith gu dé cho beag 'sa bhiodh a' rud a gheibheadh iad, 'se gini na lethghini na sòbharan na leth-sobharain a bheireadh iad seachad. 'S bha daonnan gille beag bàn còmhla riutha.

Ach, co-dhiùbh, bha cuid-eigin ann a bha . . . na b'fhiosraiche na càch agus chuir e brath air falbh agus thàinig siorram dhan dùthaich agus chaidh e dh'ionnsaigh an t-soithich aca agus thug e orra tighinn air tìr air fad, a chuile gin aca agus a' fear beag còmhla riutha. Agus thòisich . . . a' siorram air ceasnachadh an fhir bhig an toiseach, agus thuirt a' fear beag . . . 's thoisich e air caoineadh – 'Cha lig an t-eagal dhomhs' innse,' os e fhéin. 'Ach mhionnaich iad mise nach innsinn sgath is chan innis mi idir e, cha lig an t-eagal dhomh.'

'Thalla thusa,' os esan, a' siorram,' 's inns 'na' chloich mhóir ad thall e. Innis dhaibh a chuile sgath a thachair 's chan eil a chridhe aca an corra-mhèur a chur ort tuilleadh. Cha bhì turus aca riut: bidh thu air coimhead as do dheaghaidh is cha bhì sgath 'gad dhìth, agus bidh thu air coimhead as do dheaghaidh glé mhath 's cha bhi chridhe aca-san,' os esan, 'chan fhaigh iad 'nad chòir tuilleadh. Na biodh eagal 'sam bith agad romhpa.'

Is dh'fhalbh an gille beag bochd is chaidh e dh'ionnsaigh na cloiche 's dh'inns e dhan a' chloich, mar a bha facal, on iarla gos an uarla, ma dheidhinn mar a mharbh iad 'athair 's mar a chuir iad e fhéin air a mhionnan nach innseadh e sgath, 's dh'innis e chuile sgath dhaibh.

Is cha robh ach ghabhadh man cùlaibh an uair sin 's thugadh air falbh á Bhatarsaigh iad, ga brith a nist gu dé thachair dhaibh an déidh dhaibh falbh á Bhatarsaigh. Bha daoine cho fad air ais san am. Chan e cho fad air ais 's a bha iad, ach bha chuile rud cho cama-reiteach 's cha robh bàtaichean ann a bhiodh a' tighinn a seo dìreach, mar a tigeadh corra-thé dhen t-seòrs' ud fhéin air cuairt ann. Is cha d'fhuair iad a mach tuilleadh an déidh dhi . . . falbh á Bhatarsaigh, gu dé dh'eirich dhan t-soitheach a bha sin. Ach co-dhiubh bha i ann. Cha tàinig guth air . . . An fheadhainn a bha 'Bhatarsaigh a' fuireach aig an am, bha 'naidheachd aca: bhiodh an naidheachd aca riamh 'ga h-innse dhan fheadhainn eile a thainig as an deaghaidh. 'S fhad on t-saoghail on uair sin. Tha linntean . . . cinnteach gu bheil dà linn ann co-dhiùbh na trì.

The Gaelic was told second and gives fewer details of the little boy's story. The motif of telling something to an object or an animal to avoid breaking an oath not to tell it to a person is world-wide. Nan says in the Gaelic that it happened two or three centuries ago at least.

Reproduced from *Tocher* 38 1983 (SA1981/35 Bl–2).

Appendix 4: Song for the raiders

The song, written by Michael Buchanan, is introduced by Nan MacKinnon, who gives a short account of the raiding of Vatersay and her memories of moving from Kentangaval to Caolas at the age of four.

The Vatersay Raiders

I'll tell you what, when they were in Kentangaval, they hadn't a spade of earth that they could call their own. That's why they [settled] in this island. One man had the whole of this island; he had only one son. He had daughters, of course, but he had only one son. So – they lived on the rocks, that's the way. I was surprised at the tall grass [in Vatersay], and . . . there was a field of corn, and I didn't know what corn was. [In Kentangaval] I just saw a few blades of grass that were brave enough to peep through the rocks, you know. We were on the beach – we lived on the beaches there. Yes.

So, well, they took over Vatersay, and – they spent three month in Calton Jail in Edinburgh, mind you. They did, but they were set free a day before the three month were up, and they were saying – whether that's true or not – that if they had kept them in the whole time, if they had served their three month, they could have had Vatersay free of rent. That's why they set them free a day before . . .

And . . . Michael Buchanan, he was a good scholar, and a bard into the bargain, and he composed a song for them – for the Vatersay Raiders. He could speak seven languages without ever leaving Barra, before he left Barra. There was a schoolmaster in Borve, Arbuckle – he was Irish – and this Michael Buchanan, he was so brainy that he took such an interest in him, and he could speak seven languages. They were brainy, the Buchanans were supposed to be brainy right enough, and he composed a song for the Vatersay people . . .

Hù a hò gum b' éi-bhinn leam A chluinn-tinn mar a dh'éi-rich dhuibh, 'S a la-bhair thu 'n Dun-Ei - deann riu Ra - treut nach biodh 'nad cham - pa.

Hù a Hò gum B' Eibhinn Leam

Seisd:

Hù a hò gum b' eibhinn leam
A chluinntinn mar a dh' èirich dhuibh,
'S a labhair thu 'n Dun-Eideann riu
Ratreut nach biodh 'nad champa.

Tha Uilleam Baoid, gur h-airidh e
Air Beirgheaslom gu Carragraidh,
An Goirtean Geal, 's am Beannachan
Go leathad bruthach Hamhstail.

Tha Domhall Iain shìos a sin,
'S chan eil e doirbh a riarachadh:
Gu fòghnadh an Uidh Riabhach dha,
'S i math gu feurach ghamhna.

Tha Eògan ann an Eòrasdal:
O, saoil sibh nach e Toraidh e?
'S mar bi e fo lagh Dhòmhaill,
'S ann a bhòtas sinn 'n a' Ghleann e.

Tha todhar na Tràgh Tuath agaibh
A mach go Cala Shnuasamoil,
'S tha Uidh Nistean fuaighte ris,
'S an uaigh aid Mor nan Ceann ann.

Tha 'n Caolas math gubàrr agaibh:
Tha stac air Port a' Bhàt' agaibh,
'S gun cruadhaich sibh an gràn aige
'S an àthaidh a bh' aig Melvin.

A Song for the Raiders

Refrain:
What happy news for me
To hear how you fared
And how you told them plainly in Edinburgh
That there would be no retreat in your camp.

William Boyd, he ought to have
From Beirgheaslom to Caraigrigh,
The Gortein Geal, and the Beannachan
To the side of the brae of Hamhstal.

Donald John is down there,
And he's not hard to please:
The Uidh Riabhach would do fine for him,
Since it's good for grazing stirks.

Eogan there in Eorasdail,
See what a Tory he is!
And if he won't follow Donald's orders,
We'll just vote him out to the Glen.

You have seaweed rights from the North Beach
Out to Snuasimul harbour,
And Uinessan along with it,
And Mor nan Ceann's grave is there.

You have the Caolas, good arable;
You have (plenty of) drift seaweed at Port a' Bhàta,
And you can dry the grain there
In the kiln that Melvin had.

From *Tocher* 38, 1983.

Notes:

Verse 2:
Beirgheaslom: Bioruaslum
Gortein Geal: the area where the 1927 school is, and west of
there.
Hamhstal: the hillside from Gortein towards Uidh

Verse 3:
Uidh Riabhach: the Uidh peninsula west of Caraigrigh

Verse 4:
Donald: Donald MacIntyre

Verse 5:
North Beach: at Caraigrigh
Snuaisimul: a rock south-east of Uinessan
Mor nan Ceann: Morag of the Heads

Verse 6
The kiln: a kelp oven at Port a' Bhàta

Appendix 5:
Song to the *Annie Jane*

An Annie Jane

Tha brògan air Bellaig gun tarraig gun iaruinn,
Thainig a Bharraidh air cladach Tràigh Siara,
Bean Chaiptein Ros chaidh gu socair do'n t-sìorruidheachd,
Thilg iad a corp as an t-slochd roimh na ceudan.

Tha muinntir an eilein a' gèarradh nam meur dhiubh,
Gabhail na sgeanan nuair theirig na fiaclan,
Rùrach nam corp, ga robladh 's ga feuchainn,
Chì sibh mu dheireadh gun teid a'choire do'n phrìosan.

Nuair théid an Insurance an taobh seo de Alba,
Chì sibh gu sgiùrsadh gach truileach is cealgair,
'S fhalbh thus a null is thoir do chul ris a' Mheallaich,
Gheibh thu na gùin a bha aig Una 'san fhalchan.

Thàinig an *Annie Jane* a Bharraidh gun truaille,
Clann Nic Ill'Fhaolain nach do dh'innis na fhuair iad,
Luchdachadh na cairtean a' dol thairis gu Tuath leotha,
Lan fhàinichean, ghriogagan is sìoda nan uaislean.

The Annie Jane

Bella possesses shoes without nails or tackets,
Which were discovered in Barra, on the West Beach,
Captain Rose's wife who wordlessly went to Eternity,
Her body was interred in the pit, prior to the hundreds.

The inhabitants of the island dismembered the fingers,
Resorting to knives when teeth proved useless,
Ruthlessly searching and groping the bodies,
However, finally the guilty will be imprisoned.

When the Insurance visits this part of Scotland,
It is a certainty that the callous rogues will be revenged,
And if you proceed in the direction of the Meallaich,
You will find the gowns that Una had hidden.

The *Annie Jane* arrived in Barra without grief,
The MacLellans who didn't reveal all that they had discovered,
Loaded their carts and travelled to the north with them,
Laden with rings, beads and the silk of the nobility.

It is believed that this song was composed by Marion MacLean,
(Mor Chaluim Ghobha) Kentangaval, many years after the
disaster. Translation by Mary Kate MacKinnon.

Notes

Verse 1:
Captain Rose: Captain Rose was on the ship but not as Captain.
He and his wife were drowned.

Verse 3:
Insurance was the word used when referring to the Receiver of
Wrecks.
Meallaich: the name of the sandy isthmus
The Una referred to may have been the Una MacNeil who is
listed in Kentangaval Census of 1841 as being an Agricultural
Labourer, aged 40.

Part of a song to the Bermuda

Sud a *Bermuda* ùr is eireachdail
Thainig a eilein nan uaislean
Dh'fhalbh na cruinn is bhrùchd na creagan i.

There lies the *Bermuda* new and beautiful
She arrived from the island of the nobility
Her masts were shattered and the rocks damaged her.

translation by Mary Kate Mackinnon

Appendix 6: Names of children and staff in the Vatersay School photograph (plate 18)

Back Row Left to Right
Teacher Mrs Elizabeth Campbell (Ellie Eachainn), Donnie MacNeil (mac Sheumais), Peter MacNeil (mac an Dotair Ruaidh), Donald Andrew Campbell (mac Dhòmhnuill Bhig), John MacNeil (mac Eoin Dhòmhnaill Mhoir), Joseph Sinclair (mac Dhonnchaidh Mhoir), Ruairidh Iain MacNeil (Mac Sheumais Ruaidh), Calum MacDonald (mac Neckie), John Joseph Campbell (mac Dhòmhnaill Bhig), Neil MacDonald (mac an Docaidh), John Sinclair (mac Dhonnchaidh Mhoir), Head teacher Joseph Campbell (mac Iain Chaimbeul).

Middle Row Left to Right
Margaret MacLellan (Peigag Floraidh), Margaret Sinclair (ni'n Dhonnchaidh Mhoir), Isobel Campbell (ni'n Mhicheil Eachainn), Philomena Campbell (ni'n Neill Dhonnchaidh Antonaidh), Kathleen Campbell (ni'n Dhòmhnaill Bhig), Mary MacNeil (ni'n an Dollaich), Elizabeth MacNeil (ni'n Eoin

Dhòmhnaill Mhoir), Mary Sinclair (ni'n Dhonnchaidh Mhoir), Mary Elizabeth MacNeil (ni'n Dhòmhnail Bhig), Mary Ann MacNeil (ni'n Eoin Dhòmhnaill Mhoir), Philomena Sinclair (ni'n Dhonnchaidh Mhoir).

Front Row Left to Right
Malcolm Campbell (mac Mhicheil Eachainn), Duncan Campbell (mac Thomsoin), Donald D. Campbell (mac Neill Dhonnchaidh Antonaidh), Angus A. Campbell (mac Mhicheil Eachainn), Donald M. MacNeil (mac Eoin Dhòmhnaill Mhoir), Donald MacDonald (mac Neckie), Catherine MacLeod (ni'n Eoin Dhòmhnuill), Flora MacNeil (ni'n an Dotair Ruaidh), John Sinclair (mac Anndra), Michael J. MacNeil (mac Sheumais Ruaidh), Peter MacNeil (mac Sheumais Ruaidh).

Appendix 7: Glossary of Barra place-names mentioned in the text

Anglicised and Gaelic versions

Barra, Barraigh
Bentangaval, Beinn Tangabhal
Bruernish, Bruairnis
Castlebay, Bàgh a Chaisteil
Cliat, Cliaid
Craigston, Baile na Creige
Cuir, Cuithir
Eoligarry, Eòlaigearraidh
Garrygall, Gearraidh Gadhal
Glen, Gleann
Grean, Grèin
Horve, Horogh
Kentangaval, Ceann Tangabhal
Kismuil Castle, Caisteal Chiosmuil
Ledag, Leadaig
Nask, Nasg
Northbay, Bàgh a Tuath

Index